Supporting the Sense of Life

Nurturing well-being in young children and the adults who care for them

Edited by Nancy Blanning

Supporting the Sense of Life:
Nurturing well-being in young children and the adults who care for them

© 2018 Waldorf Early Childhood Association of North America

ISBN: 978-1-936849-48-2

Editor: Nancy Blanning
Copy Editor: Bill Day
Production Editor: Donna Lee Miele
Graphic Design: Amy Thesing
Cover Image: courtesy of the Hartsbrooke School, 193 Bay Rd., Hadley, MA
Images pp. 25-54 courtesy of Ruth Ker
Diagrams 1-5, 7 on pp. 97-141 courtesy of Barbara Baldwin
Image on page 141, *The Transfiguration* by Rafael: This image is in the public domain in the
U.S. and elsewhere as a photographic reproduction of a work of art in the public domain

WALDORF EARLY CHILDHOOD
ASSOCIATION OF NORTH AMERICA

Published in the United States by the Waldorf Early Childhood Association of North
America, 285 Hungry Hollow Road, Spring Valley, NY 10977
www.waldorfearlychildhood.org
Visit our online store at *store.waldorfearlychildhood.org*

This publication is made possible through a grant from the Waldorf Curriculum Fund.

Table of Contents

Table of Contents, continued

Introduction

Nancy Blanning

This book is dedicated to the sense of life: how we can understand, support, and nurture it in our children and in ourselves as the adults who care for them. When I was a child in school, this sense did not even exist! There were five senses. That was what all our school books said: touch, smell, taste, sight, and hearing. Everyone knew that. We knew that senses were real because scientific investigation—through dissecting, weighing, measuring, and so on—identified the parts of the body that did the work of sensory organs. The ear heard, the eye saw, the tongue tasted, and the nose smelled. We all knew that when we touched something, sensation followed.

But for Rudolf Steiner, sensory experience involved much more than anatomy and physiology. It led to deeply philosophical and spiritual questions: What is the true and full nature of the human being? How do we come to know ourselves, and to know the physical world through the four elements—earth, water, air, and fire—and their qualities? How do we come to know and acknowledge other people and communicate with them through thoughtful, respectful exchange? How do we make sense out of the world, and find our place in it?

Rudolf Steiner rightly understood that we have many sense experiences that the conventional five senses cannot account for. We experience ourselves inwardly; the physical, material world outwardly; and other human beings socially and spiritually. Steiner pondered these questions for thirty years before he shared his insight that twelve senses orient us in this human life. Touch, life, self movement, and balance are the foundational four senses. Then smell, taste, sight, and warmth give us experience of the outer physical world. Finally, hearing, word or language, thought, and the ability to perceive the "I" connect us with ourselves and with other human beings.

Waldorf/Steiner early childhood education supports and nurtures all twelve senses, but the first four are the primary focus of our work with children from birth to age seven. We can see from the children's behavior how secure or uncertain they feel with touch, with their own body geography and ability to move purposefully, and with physical balance. But with the life sense—which Steiner also called "the sense of well-being"—observation becomes subtle, even a little bit mysterious. Steiner said that when all is well, we do not consciously register that we even have this sensing capacity. It is only when things are out of balance that this sense awakens to let us know that we are not well, and that adjustments are needed. Especially for the young child, the nurturing and support of a healthy sense of life needs to be provided through the environment.

Our modern world is overstimulating, hurried, scattered, arrhythmic, and altogether herky-jerky. The life sense loves calmness, sensory protection, routine and order, beauty, warmth, and truthful interactions with the natural world. Children's use of technology and screens has introduced another distraction, an addictive enticement away from all the good things noted above. So how do we guide and guard our children in the face of these modern challenges?

In 2014, 2015, and 2016, the WECAN East Coast February Conference hosted presentations on "Nurturing the Sense of Life and Well-Being in Young Children and the Adults Who Care for Them." In 2014, Waldorf practitioners Susan Weber, Ruth Ker, and Patricia Rubano presented some of their practical experience in working with children, families, and adults on their developmental journeys.

Susan Weber, founder and now director emerita of Sophia's Hearth in Wilton, New Hampshire, spoke out of her experience in working with children and families in the birth-to-three setting. She opened the picture of the sense of life in describing aspects of "life forces" and "life processes" that flow in and around the life sense itself. Drawing from Rudolf Steiner and the insights of Karl König, she provided a foundation for understanding this sense. Susan described how the life sense of these vulnerable, tiny children and their families is supported by the environment we adults create as a sheltered space for the child's first years of earthly ripening. She shared that everything we do to support healthy development through nutrition, physical care, sensory protection, movement and exploration, and predictable rhythms are elevated—even spiritualized—and enriched through our intention, attentiveness, caring warmth, and joyfulness.

The next featured speaker was Ruth Ker, a long-time Waldorf early childhood educator and founding teacher of the Sunrise Waldorf School in Duncan, British Columbia, Canada. She, too, delved into the mystery of the life sense as described by Rudolf Steiner and elaborated on by Karl König and Henning Köhler. These thoughts broaden the picture of the life sense as it relates to the kindergarten-aged child (three to seven years old). The setting of the Duncan school allows for extended periods of time outdoors—working in the garden, exploring in nature, and imaginative playing in free interaction with the elements. These children get to revel in dirt, puddles, and mud; lift and tote wood for building; pull heavily laden wagons; and use wheelbarrows for hauling. Not all of our settings are so fortunate as to have such access to the outdoors. The point is that contact with the natural world, no matter how we manage it in rural or urban settings, is an important supporter of a vital sense of life.

Finally, Patricia Rubano took a biographical leap in both time and imagination. The sense of life is foundational for every human being through the whole of life. Patricia, with many years' experience in the early childhood classroom, now focuses on biography work with adults as the director of the Center for Biography and Social Art. How do we, as adult educators, support the health our own life sense in the unfolding of our personal biographies? Entering the hall wearing a donkey's ears and tail, Patricia treated everyone to a consideration of the Brothers Grimm fairy tale, "The Donkey," which had been presented in eurythmy the previous evening. We were challenged to follow the donkey's journey and consider parallels to our own life paths. The care and development of our own life sense has implications for how we can understand others in human encounters and grow a healthy social life (each of the four foundational senses corresponds to a higher social sense; the life sense corresponds to the sense of thought). Going "up hill and down" with the donkey, and coming to a kingdom where we can find expression of our true self, offered practical advice on the archetypal journey to finding self.

This theme was continued at the 2015 conference by keynote presenter Adam Blanning. As an anthroposophic family physician with a private practice in Denver, Colorado, Adam acts as school doctor for area Waldorf schools, and trains Waldorf school doctors. Supporting the sense of life is a particular focus in anthroposophic medicine, because a healthy sense of well-being engenders an experience of safety and security in being in a physical body. Resting in this sense can provide a feeling of shelter and reassurance that life is good. But our journey to this spot of security can get sidetracked along the way. Dr. Blanning shared Rudolf Steiner's description of a pathway through the senses to get to the safety and comfort of the life sense. In following this sensory pathway, the child makes his own way toward this secure domain. Where the previous year's presentations emphasized how parents and teachers create an external environment that supports the child's life sense, Dr. Blanning outlined the inner, independent aspect of life sense development. Finding our way to well-being when the environment is less than ideal is an essential skill for all of us. We can call this self-soothing, self-regulation, self-reassurance, even self-knowledge as a step to independent personhood—a goal of Waldorf education.

In 2016, Australian curative educator and speech therapist Barbara Baldwin explored "The Life Sense from the Perspective of Point and

Periphery." For many years, Barbara has worked to build bridges between home and school, between parents and teachers. She is an expert on sensory disturbances and how they negatively affect the sense of life in vulnerable children. Her presentations introduced the concept of point and periphery, which Rudolf Steiner gave to the first curative educators. We all move between the point—being centered, focused, and contained—and the periphery—being expanded and "out"—as a normal alternation. Barbara explained that sensory development can get "stuck" in one of these two extremes. The child becomes the victim, not the villain, of what we see as misbehavior. All sensory disturbances affect the sense of life, and all disturbances to this sense affect behavior. To understand this gives us tools to view distressed children with compassion. They are trapped in their circumstance and need our understanding to create relationship and then our help to find a way forward.

Barbara gifted the conference with a wealth of information. For readers newly studying sensory disturbances, this is an enlightening and thorough introduction. Seasoned educators will find new pieces of information to expand upon the knowledge base already developed. All of us are encouraged not to rush to conclusions or judgments about any child. Look at the child's behavior through the lens of the developing senses, be they healthy or disturbed. True, warmed interest opens the door to new steps forward.

Preparing these presentations for print has been a rich and privileged experience. The progression of presenters—birth-to-three educator, kindergarten class teacher, biography counselor, physician/school doctor, and therapeutic educator—offer a panorama of the sense of life that could not have been imagined or arranged in advance. The presenters' shared devotion and dedication to protecting the health and well-being of children binds these chapters into a cohesive whole. Thanks to every one of them for generously sharing their experience, expertise, and insights. The little children in our care will benefit from what they have shared and what we take into our teaching.

1. The Elixirs of Life

Susan Weber

February 7, 2014

It is a gift to be together and launch this theme through the music we shared with Eleanor Winship with her positive joyfulness and gratitude for life—because that is really the wellspring out of which we will draw forever and ever in our work with young children.

This evening, I want to work with a picture of four elixirs of life. We speak often about the child coming to birth to live her life on earth. And we talk about all that imbues that life as the child prepares to come to earthly birth. We talk about wanting to help the child build capacities for life and we explore our biographies, our own paths of life. And I thought this might be a moment to look at these elixirs, of which I would like to imagine us to be the guardians. This is not always the picture we hold. But let us hold this picture that we have the potential to be the guardians of the elixirs of life.

The First Elixir: the life forces

The first elixir is the life forces, the forces of growth and development. They are the forces that metamorphose into thinking. We know that when our life forces aren't strong, it is not easy to think clearly. It is one of the first signs for us as adults when our life forces are reduced, that thoughts just don't come in the same way. So we have to seek resuscitation, rejuvenation of our life forces. These are forces in us that we also see around the child. They support the child as he is growing and developing. As early childhood educators it is a primary task to nurture the life forces of the child. Edmond Schoorel describes the etheric body as the blueprint that the child fills in as he takes hold of his body.[1] These are also referred to as the *etheric forces.* The younger the child, the more delicate the care will be.

The Second Elixir: the life processes

The second elixir of which we are the guardians is the life processes. Rudolf Steiner did not say a lot about the life processes. He wrote about it a little bit here and there in the lectures, *The Riddle of Humanity*[2], and in *Anthroposophy—A Fragment*[3], as well. But it was Karl König who took up this work with the life processes actively and developed insights and applications in his own work with young children.[4]

König described the life processes as a ladder. In the world of the senses, we often have a picture of the senses configured as a circle. We have the sense organs, some more easily isolated and defined than others. But the picture is of a circle with each sense having its own realm and its own domain. When we explore the life processes, we are looking at something that does not have fixed organs or fixed domains but that actually weave through the whole organism. They weft and weave and one process can be layered upon top of another. Let's walk through this seven-fold picture of the life processes. Then we can explore some examples of how we might see them play out in the very young child. We hope that we might be stimulated to look for places, with the children in our care and within our activity, where we can see these life processes in action. We hope we can begin to see in a pedagogical way how we can support them to bring even more well-being to the child.

The first process that Rudolf Steiner describes, and Karl König expands upon, is *breathing*. It is interesting that in *Foundations of Human Experience*[5] and in other places, Steiner describes our task as teachers as teaching the child to breathe. Karl König describes this breathing in the life processes domain as the creation of an umbilical cord between the child and the earth. We can picture this umbilical cord in prenatal development very clearly in a physical way. Now we have the picture that after birth, the child needs to develop his tie to the earth, an umbilical cord through which nourishment comes, and also through which breathing comes. And this is possible through the support of this living, weaving life process. One could say here, that in these first life processes, this is the place where the adult is the most powerfully and especially active. The younger the child, the more this is so. We know that the young child has barely begun to create this weaving back-and-forth with the earth to enable the physiology to unfold. He needs all of our care, support, and attention. This first breathing to create the umbilical cord with the earth is, of course, the literal breathing of the air coming in and out. And we can imagine that the mantle we create around the child, this relationship with the child, enables the child to breathe. The child can feel safe, secure, and comfortable. And he can take this step into life, to say "yes" to earth life. He can breathe this "yes" in and then breathe it out to say "yes" again.

The second life process is the *warmth process*. We know that the human being requires his own activity to maintain and sustain the proper degree of warmth. If we look outside right now, it is very cold. If we followed the inclination of what it is like outside, we would become much too cold, so we have to have our own activity. This development of capacity for developing one's own inner warmth is a very slow process. We know that this is not even complete in the first seven years. We want to create a mantle around this second process, which is necessary for sustaining life and well-being, this warming process, to protect and strengthen the child.

We also notice this in particular examples. The baby's food has to be the right temperature. Why is breast milk the perfect food? It is just the right temperature. The infant has a very narrow tolerance for how warm or cold his food is. An attentive caregiver knows each child's temperature preference. Knowing what best serves each individual child is part of the activity we can do to help each child adapt to the outer world and its environment.

The third process brings the child even further "in," and this is the process of *nourishing*. Karl König uses the phrase "nourishing nutrition and nutritional nourishment." We know that we would also consider sensory nourishment, not only the nutritional nourishment of foodstuffs.

But if all we did was to take in nourishment, we would become giants. We have to let some of it go. We have to discern and discriminate what of the nourishment to keep to build up our bodily organism and what to excrete. Rudolf Steiner sometimes works with this process, calling it *secretion*. In the digestive process, first the salivary glands become active. Then, further down the digestive tract, our other digestive glands and organs become active. We sort out what stays and what goes. How do we know if an infant is healthy? We can tell by the number of wet diapers in the day whether the excreting, sorting process is working rightly. We know that many children today carry the burden of constipation. In this case the sorting and discernment process isn't quite as strong as it needs to be.

So we can see that breathing is totally an exchange of the world-out and the world-in. Then, we build up warming around the child. Nourishment literally comes into the child. The sorting and discernment become active. With each of the activities, the child is actually taking hold. These things come from the outside, but there is also life process activity internally, and the newborn baby hardly has the possibility for this activity yet. This is where we observe colic, belly cramps, crying, and other expressions of discomfort. Digestion is the hardest thing for the baby to do.

All this work that the adult does around the child in developing rhythm, warmth, and care, if we are attuned and sensitive, creates a huge support for the child. The life processes are not in boxes and separated out like the sense organs—sight, taste, hearing. They are weaving, moving, and flowing *through* the sense organs, so that even within the sense organs we can see where these life processes actually express themselves in each of the sensory activities.

As we move through the column or ladder of the life processes, as the sorting process unfolds, the body holds on to the remainder after the bowel discards what is not needed. This enables the child to *maintain* herself. This is the maintenance phase or process: finding a balance between taking in and releasing, or sending away, what is not needed. The infant and young child is very close to the hunger experience, and cannot maintain herself when nourishment is not provided in a timely way. We see this in our classrooms. If, for instance, we are a little delayed in getting snack ready for the children, the children will begin to show us through their behavior that they cannot *maintain* any longer. They need nourishment to help build something up for themselves to continue with their day.

Then comes the process of *growing*. Maintenance is not enough; otherwise, the child would remain a newborn forever. For the child the process of *growing* is critical. Regardless of whatever else is happening with the young child, he is always growing.

The final life process of the seven is *reproducing and creating anew.* Obviously, the adult is active in the procreation of children. But also, when we translate these life processes into our inner activity as adults, then we are creator-beings and we create something new that arises out of this series of processes. In the growing child in the first seven years, *play* is a powerful expression of creating.

Here is an example of how these life processes might look in the infant. Picture a baby who is just beginning to be mobile, maybe rolling from side to side, moving into side-lying and balancing on the side with one hand out. Maybe one leg is able to move freely while the child has enough balance to do this. If we think of this in terms of these life processes, we could think the first process of breathing with the world, this creation of an umbilical cord, may perhaps be the adult breathing the environment around the child so that the child feels secure and safe and ready to be active.

And then the warming step could be the adult creating those conditions around the child where the child feels comfortable, is dressed warmly, and has a warm place to freely initiate his own bodily exploration of his environment. And then the nourishment for the child is not the literal nutritional picture, per se, but is the nourishment received through the stimulation of exploring his surroundings. This nourishment comes from reaching the hand here, touching a toy there, rolling again, and always being able to move freely to nourish himself through his own self-initiated activity. Through the activity comes sorting. He might try to get into a balanced position one way; he might try a hundred times.

Then he *discards* the ways of moving that did not work. He practices and practices, discarding what doesn't work developmentally for his body and his growth and unfolding. And he tries something new. And interestingly enough, Anna Tardos, Emmi Pikler's daughter, described in her observations that for the infant, 90 percent of the movement activity would be what the child has already integrated and only 10 percent would be new. This is helpful and interesting, because we are always naturally looking for what the child is learning that is *new*. In family life and in culture we are looking for what the child can master that is new. Yet here is a picture that the child has to use 90 percent of what he has already learned and integrated in his activity for the life process of maintaining. And only a small percent is directed to exploring something new. The process of maintaining is served when the child is permitted to practice what she already knows. Being allowed to practice what she already knows is part of this process of maintaining. Out of the maintaining and finding some ability to know what is needed and what is not needed and to let go allows the possibility to grow.

The baby grows into new capacities. One of the things that happens in this sorting-discriminating-maintaining process is the integration of the primitive reflexes. The primitive reflexes have to be "sorted" away so that something else can enter in. That something else is what is maintained by the child.

With these examples, we begin to develop a picture of the sequence of these processes. Through all of this the child is growing. We could perhaps even say—and this is left to us all for our research—that there is something that is reproduced as the child masters new capacities. We can see that when the second half of these seven-fold processes actually rises up, the child is offering something back to life. With the first half, something is coming toward the child from the outside. Then with the second half, it is as though there is an involuted spiral and something reaches back out as the child offers his own being to the universe.

Rudolf Steiner says that these life processes are not organs of perception. Hopefully we can feel that through this consideration. These are feeling-like, instinctive experiences. These life processes are *below* the level of sense perception. They are much less conscious. They are moving and active but at a deeper level inside the human being. We could imagine that since they are seven-fold, there would be a relationship to the astral body. In fact, Rudolf Steiner describes that this is so, that these seven-fold processes do bear a relationship to the astral body that one can explore further.

We can see that if we are with children in the first three years in particular, we need to work with the life processes in such a way that the child has movement that engages the whole body, so that the life process can flow through movement. We need nutrition, we need warmth. These are all things we think about in rhythm and care-giving with the young child. They also come to mind as we envision the physical environment for the baby and young child. These also become markers for our use of the picture of the life processes as a support for the child's growth as well. The child has to be able to experiment and make things his own and turn things inside out. We can see that these processes have a time element. For the fullness of health and well-being in the child to truly manifest, it is crucial that enough time is allowed for each process. The processes must not be truncated, collapsed, or contracted, but allowed enough time to flow one into the next, into the next, so they can adequately live in their rightfulness. We want to take this up as our research to see where we can explore the activity of these life processes in our own situations. Where do we see the essential activity coming from the adults? Where do we see the children manifest these processes themselves?

Karl König says that the twelve senses are a frame, so to speak. Within the twelve senses, the seven living processes move and weave. It is not a form we are considering here. Therefore, it is not anatomy or morphology or physiology as we understand it today. It is living, weaving etheric being. It is this second elixir of life, the life forces, that we can point to so we can make this picture a tool for our insight.

The Third Elixir: the sense of life

The third elixir is the sense of life. This is the "happy" sense, as described by Karl König.[6] It is the sense of well-being. It is *not* an alarm system that tells us that we are coming down with a sore throat. This is not the sense of life. Falling ill is a picture of my life forces diminishing. But the life sense itself is a mirroring of well-being. We all know that for some children this is challenging process.

> By means of the sense of life, the human being learns to experience himself as a complete within-ness and senses himself as a bodily self, filling space. The body becomes mine through the sense of life. The sense of life gives us security in our earthly existence. The sense of life spreads its blanket of sensations over the life processes in the body.[7]

Rudolf Steiner said that if we bought a pair of gloves that fit as badly as our physical body fits our soul and spirit, we would throw the gloves away.[8] This is true for everyone to some degree. But we know children for whom this is especially true. This third elixir, the sense of life, mirrors what is happening under the surface, within our sense of well-being. When all is calm, the lake's surface is unbroken. When we think of distressed children, we can picture that some of them are like a shattered mirror or a disturbed lake. They are absolutely uncomfortable in their bodies much of the time. This calm mirroring that we hope for—that one's body is a good place to be, is comfortable to be in, and is a place in which the child wants to be active—is not present for them.

The organ of the sense of life is the sympathetic nervous system, and it requires nine months to mature adequately so that the child can "tolerate" his organ system.[9]

The following example of a specific child will give us a picture of this mirror being shattered, and then beginning to be healed through days and weeks of life experience. A little girl came to Sophia's Hearth. She had been sent away from another childcare program. She was just two years old. She had been sent away because she was crying—screaming—all day long. The caregivers could not calm her. They didn't have a ratio that would enable someone to be with her in even her most delicate times to try to bring her solace. She came to Sophia's Hearth and cried and screamed and screamed so much that the caregivers' ears were over-stimulated and they had to move out of the space with her. The question had to be seriously considered as to whether they could meet this child. We can imagine the mother's anxiety. There was not much of anywhere else to go after Sophia's Hearth. The most challenging time of the day was at nap time. This child could not even lie down on her mat. She would sit and cry. She would be walked in the hall in someone's arms so the other children could sleep. This went on and on from August into the fall. The crying diminished. When they would talk to the mother, they could see her anxiety.

Time went on. Thanksgiving came and the child had nearly stopped crying. The caregivers noticed that the first sign of this mirror being restored was not the cessation of the crying but through her showing that she was making a home in this place and her body by beginning to name the other children. It was not long before she could name every child. And that then moved forward to her going to the bathroom where she knew which hand cloth belonged to every child. Even in this grieving and incredible pain, she was still taking something in. She is now about two and a half years old. She has just started saying "I" to herself. And she asked to have her bread buttered on both top and bottom.

The other thing that is interesting is that this was a child with extended breast feeding. Karl König's and Edmond Schoorel's[10] observation is that the life sense does not become truly active until the child is weaned—we might consider this at least nine months old. There is in their work the suggestion that there may be a relationship between weaning and the healthy manifestation of the life sense.

We have a picture of the lake reflecting. If we have life processes not doing well under the surface, how will the mirror be? Cloudy, cracked, smudgy. It won't be very nice. The feeling for the child of "here I am at home in my body" cannot yet quite rise. This sense of life is truly a sign, when we see it in a joyful, healthy way, that all is right in the world for that child in this moment.

We can see that the sense organs are developing for the child in these early years. We observe that everything has a slow ripening period. Life processes mature unevenly and slowly. We may be able to see, as we can how a child's senses are maturing, how these life processes are maturing as well. We can begin to see how each of these processes is coming to expression through a deepening of our work with rhythm. I wonder if there is a way to refine our work in the classroom so we can see within our rhythm how the life process is developing and is active!

The Sacramental Path

When we work with the life substance, we are working with something that is sacramental, and we unite the eternal with the transitory. *Life* is the sacred substance of our work. We can think about a healing substance as a substance that has been humanized. When we work in a sacramental way, we humanize and spiritualize the material world around us. We transform substance so that it can touch the child and heal the child. In these first three years, we have the possibility to spiritualize all of the substances—nutritional substances, for example—with our intention, with our attentiveness, with our care, and with our joy.

We can take hold of the simplest activity that we do with the child. The diaper can be spiritualized. The placing of the bib, helping with a mitten, cutting an apple can each become a spiritual deed. In all these ways we sacramentalize the life with which we work. With our healing activity and substances, we humanize our vocation. We provide the child with a growing sense of security in which the mirror of the life sense becomes calmer, more still, and reflective of the goodness of the world.

If we apply these life-bearing substances to the child, the child will, in his way as he can in time, become filled with life. He will become active within the unfolding of his destiny. This mirror of the sense of life will become calmer and more still and reflective. The more we work as Rudolf Steiner has described, as priests and priestesses in our work, the more we take up this possibility of humanizing matter, miracles will occur. In our times there is probably nothing that we are called upon to do more deeply than to humanize the world around us. It is *only* the human encounter that can heal.

We are learning this more and more every day: that the adversarial elements around us are simply there to point us to doing the good. It is our invitation to see the good, to say I recognize you, I can name you. And I am moving in this direction to humanize everything I touch. For every human encounter I will try to be as present as I possibly can. That we can fill ourselves with this joy, to have this picture that we can radiate to the children—"I am joyful to be with you. I am joyful to follow the steps of your journey with my own being and with my heart. I am joyful to get to know the mystery of who you are." Clearly this is what the parents are asking of us as well. Not just that we ask them to know about warmth and nutrition, but that we say to them, "I am interested in who you are. What is your path? What do you care about? Who are you trying to become?" We want to have joy and interest in this encounter that radiates our well-being. And we become the models of this well-being for the child. We have all heard the following quotation from Rudolf Steiner's *Education of the Child in the Light of Anthroposophy.* The question is how to make it more active:

> The joy of children in and with their environment must, therefore, be counted among the forces that build and shape the physical organs. They need teachers that look and act with happiness [the life sense] and most of all with honest, unaffected love. Such a love that streams, as it were, with warmth through the physical environment of the children. Pleasure and delight are the forces that most properly enliven and call forth the organs' physical forms. It may be said to literally hatch the forms of the physical organ.[11]

Over and over again we hear "pleasure," "delight," and "joy"—not anxiety and worry, but positive picturing and radiating to the child all that is possible from our hearts and souls as we work with them.

The Fourth Elixir: the Christ forces

This brings us to the fourth elixir of life, the wellspring that never runs dry. It is the wellspring we read of in the gospels, the water of life that will never cease to flow. These are the Christ forces. If we can find in ourselves a relationship to those forces, we will have the possibility to live into our work and with all the children, families, and colleagues around us with something that will, step by step, radiate joy and well-being out into their world.

NOTES

1. Edmond Schoorel, *The First Seven Years: Physiology of Childhood* (Fair Oaks, California: Rudolf Steiner College Press, 2005), p. 79.

2. Rudolf Steiner, *The Riddle of Humanity: The Spiritual Background of Human History* (Forest Row, UK: Steiner Press, 1990).

3. Rudolf Steiner, *Anthroposophy (A Fragment)* (Hudson, New York: Anthroposophic Press, 1996).

4. See, e.g., Karl König, *A Living Physiology* (Bolton Village, UK: Camphill Books, 1999).

5. Rudolf Steiner, *Foundations of Human Experience* (Hudson, New York: Anthroposophic Press, 1996).

6. König, *A Living Physiology* at 178.

7. Ibid.

8. Rudolf Steiner, *The Kingdom of Childhood* (Hudson, New York: Anthroposophic Press, 1995) page 9.

9. König, *A Living Physiology* at 191.

10. Schoorel, *The First Seven Years* at 134-38.

11. Rudolf Steiner, *Education of the Child in the Light of Anthroposophy* (Forest Row, UK: Rudolf Steiner Press, 1981), p. 22.

Supporting the Sense of Life

2. Observing Life Sense Development

Ruth Ker

February 8, 2014

Karl König's image of the healthy life sense as a smooth, mirroring, reflective lake[1] is helpful when we contemplate what could bring disturbances or ripples to the sanctity of our life senses. The life sense is in its element, and the human being feels that "all is well," when this pool is calm and still. Standing before all of you in this big hall is a scary place for me and I'm guessing that my life sense has a rippled surface right now. Sometimes we can also observe or hear from the children how their life sense is informing them.

The Early Childhood Setting: One of the best research environments

Often the children have reactions or say things and, if we are truly present with them, we can pick up the cues they are giving us. I'm remembering some recent occurrences.

Here's one story. Our school, located on the edge of farmland, provides the opportunity for the children to play on the hill overlooking the farmer's tree-lined fields. One day the farmer had a large, smoky fire burning, and as the smoke wafted up to the playground, it became obvious that the children were becoming increasingly agitated and restless. Wearing a worried expression, finally one little boy said, "Ruth, I can't seem to find the good air. It's not here today!" In this situation, it became evident that the compromised air quality unconsciously affected the sense of well-being of the whole group. There were eighteen little rippling lakes that day!

Another time, I escorted a little girl to the bathroom from the place where we have our daily walk. Because it was closer, I took her down to the grade school bathroom in the main school. From the moment we entered the unfamiliar bathroom, she showed signs of agitation and wanted to leave. I modeled what we do there by washing my hands and going to the paper towel dispenser. At this point she showed even more signs of distress and began backing away. I pulled down the lever of the paper towel dispenser and out came the paper towel. The little girl, gasping with obvious relief, said, "Thank goodness it isn't one of those windy ones! I'm scared of them." Later her mother confirmed for me that she was frightened by the air-blowing hand dryers in bathrooms.

Children are exposed to many new experiences every day. When we seriously try to put ourselves in the child's place, there are frequent occurrences that have the potential to cause ripples in that place of calmness—that still, calm pool.

So let's take some time to strengthen our understanding of the life sense so that we can be more attuned to our children's experiences when we return to our classrooms. We can glean many insights by consulting some of the inspirational thinkers of our time.

Goethe said that we can always trust our senses and that they tell us the truth, but our reasoning confuses matters. Rudolf Steiner quoted Goethe and went on to say, "The life sense is something in the human being, that if everything is in order, he actually does not notice, something that he or she only notices if something in the human being is not in order."[2]

In our times, the life sense receives almost no attention in mainstream research. Fortunately, we have much spiritual-scientific research to call upon and I hope you will permit me to share some of this today as we further our understanding together.

Rudolf Steiner tells us that it is the sense of life radiating into the soul that makes it possible for us to be inwardly aware of ourselves as a self-enclosed, living bodily totality.[3] He also called it life feeling. The sense of life works dimly within the organism but, whenever anything is upset, then our life sense informs our feelings that something is amiss.

Just as the sense of touch can help us to have trust in "the other" and ultimately, trust in God, the sense of life can help us to have a sense of well-being in our earthly bodily home. We can feel at home on earth—our soul has an anchor in this earthly reality. These two senses make it possible for the child, and ultimately the adult, to be a resident in both worlds—to feel safe and at home with heaven and earth.

For the newborn, the life sense is still developing and the harmonious interaction of all the organs that eventually can lead to a sense of well-being is still in flux. Little children are consumed by what is happening with their organs and overwhelmed by the newness of their physical body to life. Many disturbances, large and small, can cause ripples on this mirroring lake that Karl König describes.

Rudolf Steiner spoke about the life sense in a few places. In 1909, he said that the life sense facilitates us having the first human perception of "self," the first time that we experience ourselves as a body. He filled out the picture eleven years later, in the 1920s, when he said that the life sense is a general *feeling* of oneself. "We could not know ourselves as being a bodily self in space if we did not have the activity of the sense of life radiating into the soul."[4] The life sense helps us to know when we are hungry, thirsty, tired, and so on. We would also be unaware of the flow of life and even be unable to sense into our own biography if we did not have this life sense within us.

This inward sensing connected to the whole body is what Willi Aeppli simply calls "Undefined…through this sense we go most deeply into ourselves and experience through it our physical existence."[5] Karl König tells us that these feelings are dimly recognizable, barely rise to our consciousness, and mingle with other sense impressions and feelings. Nevertheless, they "give our soul its anchor in this earthly reality where it is a stranger." He says, "The body becomes mine through the sense of life."[6]

A lot of us associate the sense of life with vitality, but Henning Köhler asks us not to confuse these two things. Vitality is an awakeness, a liveliness, an energetic state. The sense of life informs us that that our body is energized, but it plays the role of *mirroring* the bodily state. What it is really telling us is that deep down inside, the sense of life is feeling peace and warmth and well-being when our organism is in vital health.[7] Interestingly, two other names that Rudolf Steiner called the sense of life are "the vital sense" and "the feeling-life sense."

The life sense has an intimate relationship with the etheric body.

Rudolf Steiner speaks about supersensible processes guided by high spiritual beings that are inherent in the forming of our sense organs. Then, specifically about the sense of life, he says:

> The physical and etheric bodies cooperate to help the sense of life develop. It is a certain mutual relationship whereby something new occurs in the etheric body. Something that is different permeates and flows through the etheric body and saturates it, just like a sponge. It is bestowed upon him by the surrounding, outer spiritual world without his being able to participate in it. In the distant future, humanity will have developed it within themselves. And that which is saturating the etheric body, coming from without, is Spirit Man.[8]

Steiner emphasizes that we are not ready to do this for ourselves yet; but in the future, we will be.

How do these processes allow our sense of life to inform us about where we are with our own well-being? To paraphrase: unconsciously, Spirit Man expresses itself by contracting the etheric. When this happens, our astral body is squeezed right out. Then, because the etheric is compressed, the physical undergoes tension. And when this tension happens, the astral slips right back in and then this is when we can have the experience, the feeling through the astral body, of the bubbling up of the feeling life radiating into the soul.[9] This cooperative process informs us about what is going on with our state of being because it is mirrored by the life sense. We can be grateful for the work of the spiritual beings who have been involved in these supersensible processes within us.

As the life sense develops—and it does take a while for this to happen—what the human being experiences is just a dimly felt recognition of bodily sensations. This developing life sense later allows us, as adults, to have a sense of our own biography. We can have the feeling that life flows and that situations connect with one another because our sense of life has helped us put things together in regular rhythms and routines.

As educators, we can inwardly sense into the biography of the child as well. You might be familiar with the quotation from *Education as a Source for Social Change* where Steiner said that educators, who are in service to the child's future, can perceive "each child as a question posed by the supersensible world to the sense-perceptible world."[10] As teachers, this is a powerful thing to remember. We can be more effective in our work if we can stand in awareness of our own biography and also be able to carry this question about the children. Educators and parents, while carrying these important destiny questions, do well to also be attentive in the moment to what is going on for the child in his organism. The signals arising from the child's life sense as it mirrors an inner disturbance provide us cues that we can observe with discerning eyes.

Children tend to be united with the moment, so when there are sensory or organ disturbances—and there are many because children are so vulnerable while building their bodies—it is not always possible for them to express what's going on or to remedy a situation themselves. Our presence is important. Let's imagine being seasick…everything is topsy-turvy. Even in the midst of this distress adults can still ask themselves, "How do I take hold of my organism again?" We know that we will probably feel better when the sea stops rolling. It is very different for young children, who are engaged with their whole being in what is happening in the moment. Their total engagement often does not involve knowing how to get out of the situation; they need our help. They need our compassionate presence and the assurance that we will take charge to help them. The possibility of these kind and trusting relationships can help the young child build a positive picture around what life is really like. The child can have the unconscious assurance that "life is full of good people who care for me and help me."

How can we support the health of the developing life sense?

Anything that supports the healthy etheric body—rhythm, good food, sleep, exercise, experiences in nature—also supports the life sense.

Protection of the life sense of the developing child is important for their future well-being. We can read more about this in Henning Köhler's book, *Working with Anxious, Nervous and Depressed Children*, where he equates restlessness and nervousness with outer signs of life sense disturbances.[11] Some things that can strengthen the child's feeling of well-being and life sense, and ultimately his etheric body, are safeguarding healthy approaches to diet; providing rhythmic regularity and order; giving appropriate praise; allowing appropriate exposure to death; offering regular contact with nature; humor; modeling tolerance and responsible processes; providing games and non-moralizing stories that embrace simple justice and fairness.

When the sense organs are developing, children need rest. The sense organs actually begin to develop in the embryo. At this time, they are very fragile, very new. If we don't use these sense organs, they will atrophy. The sense organs are meant to be used, but used in the right way. In order to refresh them, they need rest. Sleep supports the health of the life sense in the child and the adult. The life sense loves the settled feeling we experience when we are on the edge of sleepiness. If you want to get to know the life sense in yourself, this is where you can start your phenomenological research. Then take time to consider how different most children's worlds are from this edge of sleepiness. We make many excuses to not take time to rest or take a break or even to go to sleep on time. In our school communities we see many sleep disturbances in the children and also have the experience of parents rushing to the door, dropping the child off and leaving in a hurry. Often, after inadequate sleep, the child is caught in the midst of this haste—a far step away from the edge of sleepiness.

Now, we can ask ourselves, "How do I receive the children so they can find their way back to this dreamy, sleepy condition that is supportive of the life sense?" In our own practices, it is very important for us, as teachers, to get to school on time—ideally even early. This is so we can ensoul the room beforehand and then be ready and prepared so that we can consciously receive the children on these home/school thresholds. Our well-traveled colleague Louise deForest recommends that we spend time straightening up the environment and, even, touching the toys before school starts. She says that the children can feel this caring gesture of the teacher who has endowed the environment with this attention and intention beforehand. It is better for the children if they are interfacing with a relaxed ambience in the early childhood classroom rather than sensing that the teacher is running around the room getting things together at the last minute.

An anthroposophical nurse living in my community once told a personal story that demonstrates the value of rest for the life sense. When she was ill as a child, her mother would create a "nest" in her bed, keep her home, and give her ample time to recuperate, often at least one week. When she was telling a group of parents in the Waldorf school about this, the looks on parents' faces reflected how odd they thought this was. Then the nurse told the parents about going through a major illness and staying in her bed for two weeks. She talked about this "nest" becoming something akin to a sacred space for her. It was a place where she had really gone through something, a transformation had happened in that special place. And when her mother told her it was time to leave her bed, she felt reluctant to leave behind the place where she had gained strength and come into herself. She said she had a dim sensing that when she left this, she could not go back to this same experience again. She knew it was possible that she might be in the same recuperation bed again, but she would be a different person when that happened the next time. The parents' reactions to this story confirmed how foreign this idea was to their modern experience. After this advice from the nurse, though, I noticed that more parents were able to give their children extra time to rest and recuperate from their illnesses.

Rhythm and routine are instrumental for the development of a healthy sense of life. The feeling that "all is well" flourishes when things happen with continuity, when events have rhythm and regularity. Then, with this guarantee of few variations in routine, there are fewer life sense upsets that bubble up for the children. The children can rely on this regularity and the security that there will be few changes. In our early childhood classrooms, we know well the "rippling wind" that blows through the group if something happens out of order.

What are the organs for the life sense?

The autonomic nervous system (ANS), sometimes called the vegetative nervous system, is the main organ for the sense of life. The ANS, which develops gradually in the first few years of life, is composed of parts called the sympathetic and parasympathetic. These two operate with mutuality and are all about cooperative intervals of activity and rest. This gives us another picture for the sense of life. The sympathetic nervous system (SNS) and parasympathetic nervous system (PNS) cooperate and gradually, as the child grows, begin to do amazing things. The SNS is predominantly responsible for helping to develop and sustain and inform the sense of life.

The PNS is what begins to develop, at about age three, into the inklings of the sense of thought. We might also remember that Steiner tells us that the sense of life prepares for the development of the sense of thought. Karl König tells us that "in the third year of the child's development, the skill of forming thoughts awakens."[12] Three is quite a threshold when we think about all that happens at that age! The sense of thought has tender beginnings already at three. It is also about this time in the child's biography that he designates himself as "I." This is a time when the children also begin to ask very interesting questions.

A memory comes to mind of being at the seashore with my husband and son, then almost three. We went out onto the balcony of our room and were looking out at the sea where the waves were rolling in. Of course, when there is wind, there will be spray on the crest of the waves. We could also see the waves pulling sand back from the shoreline. My son was speechless with wonder for a long while and then asked what was happening. His father gave an explanation of the pressure of the water that was pulling the sand back and the wind that was blowing the waves. The explanation was interrupted by the child needing to use the bathroom, allowing an escape from this factual explanation. As we left, my son pulled on my skirt and seriously asked, "Mom, do water fairies have hair?" One can see the emergence of the sense of thought, accompanied by lush images in this example.

Gradually in the child's life the sympathetic nervous system takes on the function of sense organ for the sense of life and the upper parasympathetic nervous system slowly takes on that function for the sense of thought. How precious it is that we can, through supporting the development of these systems, help the human being to be able to eventually listen to what is behind the word; to actually communicate with people and not just hear the words but the thoughts behind what is being said. This tender framework is already beginning its development when the child is three! This means that, supporting the physical body's possibility to have health allows the human being to later on find meaning in life. Rudolf Steiner takes a step further in the importance of health in an individual's sense of life when he says that "the sense of life expresses itself in later life as a basic feeling of our inner life."[13]

I was initially trained in mainstream education. Teachers were taught to look for the moment when the child expressed what seemed like a thought. And then we were instructed to begin "picking at the child's words," asking questions, and honing in on intelligent answers. However, what children really need is time to wonder and, if any answers are warranted, then to be provided with open-ended, magical responses. Every opportunity for the children to respond to something greater than dry, intellectual words, stripped bare of imagery, helps the children to sink into the magical land of wonder that they deeply crave. If we truly listen to young children, they will show us what answers are needed.

A scenario comes to mind. One day I came upon two children, a boy and girl, from different families, together in the playground where a group of friends were gathering around them. I had already learned that the boy's father gave lots of intellectual answers to his questions and the girl was left more free to wonder. I saw the girl in tears and went to investigate what the trouble was. The little girl was proclaiming, "He is not! Father Sun is not like that." And the boy was insisting, "He's just a ball of gases. My Dad told me!" The children around were full of angst about all of this. Then finally one of the other children asked, "How does he get his gases?" And the boy replied, "Silly! You know those pipes that come out from cars? The gases just drift up and he grabs them." Having said this, all of the children seemed satisfied, whereupon they dispersed and continued playing together. One can see that, even though his father had given him explanations devoid of pictures, this boy had managed to transform his words into a lively picture. His peers were not satisfied with the father's explanation either until they heard the fanciful picture his son had reconciled.

As adults we can contribute to the child's healthy life sense by trying our best to bring goodness into these explanations and soften these intellectual pictures that the children have been given. The possibility of imaginative outcome, full of goodness, gives the children a sense of well-being. It contributes to the "all-is-well" condition in their life sense. If we listen to the children, we can see that some of those intellectual things the children hear are then transformed into a picture that is more easily digested by them. We can help the children with this by supporting these magical pictures, and even bringing them into our circles and nature stories. Perhaps the children have something to teach us about forming picture imaginations.

WECAN has published a collection of Rudolf Steiner's quotes about the threshold that bridges the kindergarten into the grade school years. It's called *From Kindergarten into the Grades*.[14] Reading it, I am struck by the number of times Rudolf Steiner mentions the importance of the educator working on herself so that she can have the inheritance of the pictures to share with the children. He brings this up over and over again. He also says in almost every lecture that educators need to take strides to develop the extra sense organs that are needed to sense into these things, to evolve what has been given to us in order to develop extra soul-spiritual capacities within ourselves.

How can we actively set about developing our own soul-spiritual capacities?

In the course of deepening my understanding of what this sense of life is, I felt supported by the many times that Rudolf Steiner reiterates that there are spiritual forces and supersensible beings that are underlying everything we see in the world. Actually, our sense organs would not be able to exist if they did not have the support of these invisible beings working into them. Living beings work within everything that is around us. It is important that we, as educators, cultivate our respect for what the earth is and for what lies behind the sense world. Sunshine, fresh air, and nature impressions sustain, replenish and build the child's body—and our own.

In our kindergarten, we always begin the morning outside, in all weather conditions. Of course we each have our own unique situations and consequent routines. In our situation, we have noticed that, if we miss our regular two hours outside, the teachers *and* the children feel the lack in their own being—something akin to hunger, a certain restlessness and yearning for the missing nourishment. This time in outside play gives something supportive to everyone. This is also a place where we can have daily interplay with those beings who make themselves available and assist in sensitizing the developing senses of the child and the teacher.

Our life sense is nourished by both earthly and cosmic nutrition.

What is earthly and cosmic nutrition?

Human beings depend on nutrition not only from earthly sources in our immediate environment but also from the whole cosmos. Daily food intake forms the basis for life and growth. In the same way, external stimuli and the new impressions we get from cosmic nutrition enrich our inner life and encourage spiritual growth. Both are necessary for the human being to have a sense of well-being. We can support the children's life sense by giving them healthy diets which help them to anchor their body on earth. We can also tend what Rudolf Steiner calls their feeling life sense by being attentive to the forces from the cosmos that are active everywhere.

Let us imagine now that the earth is a microcosm and cosmic space is the macrocosm around it. We can imagine that the earth is a mighty being wandering in this peripheral space and is actively collecting all the gifts and impressions from the sun, moon, and stars there. And then this earth-being brings those impressions back into herself and creatively manifests them outwardly—such as the star in the primrose or the star hidden within the apple. Let's shift this picture and suppose that there is another macrocosm, and this time it is the earth. And now the child and the teacher are the microcosm, wandering on the earth. They are also witnessing these amazing things that the earth has taken into herself—the star in the apple and in the primrose. In *The Essentials of Education,*[15] Rudolf Steiner talks about how important it is that we experience this awe and wonder with the child. It is not just an arbitrary "something" that happens in our thinking processes, there are actual spiritual substances coming to us through stopping to look and wonder and admire and "be" in the magic of this event. This transference of substance gives our thinking the possibility of nurturing the pictures for the children that they need. This is a process that it is important for us to engage with. It fuels us and gives us the possibility to create imaginative pictures for the children. These pictures are gifts from other beings that we can take into ourselves just like dear old mother earth has done.

There is another macrocosm and microcosm. If we develop the right kind of relationship with the children,[16] if we think about connecting to them, attaching to them—not the kind of attachment where we carry them around all over the place, but the kind of attachment where we sustain the connection and do not allow ourselves to break it—then the children will reveal themselves to us in the most amazing way. Then the teacher becomes the macrocosm and the children are the microcosm. Sometimes this reverses when the children come up with their amazing imaginations and we get to be the recipient.

When we then share picture imaginations out of ourselves, we see how animated the children become. Receiving these pictures just stops them in their tracks and they seem compelled to respond. We could use picture imaginations rather than, for example, saying, "Stop yelling," "It is too loud in here," "This is hurting my ears," or, as we sometimes say, "Use your inside voice." These directives have very little meaning to a child. They are empty abstractions for the child's ear. Rather, in picture-language, we could say, "My, it sounds like the squawking parrots are in the land. I wonder if Brother Robin is here somewhere?" Awakening this imaginative capacity in ourselves is hard work for us, as educators, because we have been accustomed for so long to first go to factual understandings in our thinking processes.

We can look at Nelson Mandela's autobiography, *The Long Walk to Freedom,* as we contemplate two things related to the developing life sense—the importance of children having nature experiences and the adults in their life whom they are drawn to emulate. Mandela writes about his amazing childhood, where he played on the veld every day, his parents unaware of his whereabouts. He and his friends would compose their own expansive plays and hack branches and pretend that they were oxen and they would slide down the clay hills until their backsides ached.[17] They would play to their hearts' content all day long. When this picture was shared with a kindergarten colleague, she—an adult known for her sweetness and gentleness—shared that when she was a child, she and her brother used to play jackals for weeks, even months. One year they played jackals all summer long. In our adult mind, we think of jackals with alarm. What this speaks to me, however, is that, in this unrestricted play, she could really play something out fully and get a sense of it. This is what Nelson Mandela was allowed to do. We can all recognize the life forces he carried through his whole biography. Even to the end of his life he seemed full of strength and purpose.

Mandela spoke of a person in his life, the Reverend Harris, a stern man who had strength of purpose. Some of his friends were afraid of Reverend Harris. But when he was in the garden, the way he was as a devoted gardener, touched Nelson Mandela deeply. Mandela said that Reverend Harris implanted within him a life-long love of gardening; standing as an example of a good man who was unselfishly devoted to a good cause. He further goes on to say of Reverend Harris that he was not someone who nurtured him but rather, it was who Reverend Harris was in his being that made the impression. And it was out of respect for this way of being that Mandela was inspired to carry this influential memory into his later life.

In 1998, a Waldorf center opened in a township in South Africa. Nelson Mandela, who was still president at that time, gave the opening address. In keeping with his oft-quoted principles about children and society, he said many things about children as both society's most vulnerable citizens and its greatest wealth.[18] Nelson Mandela most assuredly was given ample opportunity to strengthen his life forces. The results of this interplay of cosmic and earthly nutrition on this one human being benefited all of humanity.

Now let us investigate a little further how the spiritual beings participate in the building of the life sense for the child. We all take for granted that the food children eat is of great importance. The quality of nutrition is one of the first things on our lips when we think about nurturing the young child. And…there are so many alternatives these days. Perhaps you also have the experience that, on bread day, there is a plate with coconut butter and gluten-free bread. On another plate by a different child's table spot is placed only rye bread and Earth Balance—no butter. And then there is another plate with the kindergarten bread with no butter and another plate actually with bread and butter. There is quite an array these days of different dietary needs and preferences we encounter. To discuss all of this is not something we want to go into right now. But one thing I've found to be useful is to grind nuts or seeds into the snack grain to add a bit of protein. Some children have traveled quite a distance to school and then, after being outside for two hours, I want them to eat something sustaining. Something raw is always served with the grain as well. No sweetener is served; there are only some raisins to sweeten our porridge. Although initially there may be some upturned noses, eventually most children are hungrily devouring what their eighteen other classmates are eating.

Rudolf Steiner says that the food we eat affects the physical body, and it also affects our thinking and our spiritual faculties—the relationship we will have later on to thinking spiritual thoughts and to spiritual beings themselves. The food itself isn't what builds up our body. He talks about two streams. There is the stream of earthly nutrition and the stream of cosmic nutrition. When we take food in, it breaks down into little particles. Then, if we were considering the mineral substance of the food, we would see that it is actually completely destroyed in our digestive processes. After that, it becomes etherized until it becomes warmth. In that condition, it can be united with the cosmic stream of nutrition. This cosmic nutrition, in combination with this transformed earthly nutrition, is what then builds human substance.

Steiner's teachings guide anthroposophical medicine in saying that the amount of vitality in the food that we eat is extremely important.[19] If the vitality isn't there, the transformed substance composed of the union of cosmic and earthly nutrition cannot be pushed out with sufficient vigor into the limbs and into the whole body. It is imperative that the earthly nutrition the children receive be as full of life forces as possible so it can go through this rigorous transformation and still be potent enough to permeate the child's whole body.

I was pondering whether I could think of a possible relevant life experience about this phenomenon and I'm wondering if the following might be one. One year, a little boy who had been adopted from China came into our kindergarten family. In China there used to be a tendency to value boys more highly than girls. But for some reason, this boy had been kept with the girls in the orphanage. Perhaps it was because he was premature and tiny when he was born. The adoptive mother brought photos showing us how he had spent the first fourteen months of his life, propped up in one of twenty wooden cradles with forty other children, lined up in several rows in a big room.

This boy was fed gruel, and when his adoptive mother got him at age two-and-a-half, he could barely walk. When he came to the kindergarten he was still very thin, pale, and under-developed. Later, when he had played in the kindergarten for a few months, both indoors and out, he began to grow, get rosy cheeks and was able to strengthen in his belief that he could take on the same tasks as the other children. I saw him recently as a young adult and, although he is still small compared to most people his age, when we spoke, he seemed full of self-esteem and confidence that "all is well with me and the world."

For many years, I'm guessing that we have all followed the Waldorf recommendations of natural toys, natural fabrics, getting into nature, and wholesome foods. But when we understand the living forces inherent in these things, we can have deeper realizations about the benefits for the children—the soul/spiritual harvest they stand to reap from elemental substances in their outdoor and indoor play spaces. These environments and what is in them is actually building the child's bodily organism. We, as early childhood educators, have the honor of supporting the foundational sense organs simply by providing a healthy environment. This has far greater repercussions than we might realize.

It's obvious that warmth, sunlight, air, sounds, and visual impressions are all contained in the substances that come to us through cosmic nutrition. Rudolf Steiner tells us that there are also trace minerals and metallic substances that enter the earth's atmosphere from cosmic space. These are also very important for us. Earthly nutrition gives us the substances we need for building, in particular, the brain and nervous system. And it gives us the forces we need for will activity and the functioning of our metabolic organs. Cosmic nutrition gives us the substances for our metabolic organs, our muscles, and our blood, and the forces particularly for thought activity.

We have talked a bit about how the spiritual world is involved. And we also want to get very practical as well. How do the adults in the

child's life nurture her sense of the world being predictable, safe, sensible, and secure? Gordon Neufeld, a developmental psychologist from Vancouver, British Columbia, spoke of the phenomenon of increased entitlement in the "privileged" children of today—we may encounter this in our programs as well. Dr Neufeld encourages parents and educators to strengthen the resilience and security of the children by providing reliable firm boundaries. He gives the familiar scenario of the child coming home after school and wanting a cookie before dinner. He emphasizes to parents that, if it is the family rule that there is no cookie before dinner, the parents should not give in. He says that children need to meet "the wall of futility." This prepares them to be resilient in a world that does not mirror flexible laws. He says that parents and educators need to be double agents—angels of comfort and angels of futility. In the kindergarten, as we work out of imitation, sometimes we have to firmly bring the children along with us until they can imitate us. And there are times when we do have to give the children the "gift of no."[20]

What other things can educators do to consciously nourish the life sense?

1. The purposeful, meaningful activity of the teacher gives the child a sense of well-being. When we are on the playground, we need to be active, not standing idle or talking with our colleagues.

Our kindergarten has its own garden plot that the kindergarteners take care of all year. If the teacher lays down a tool, a child is likely to pick it up and run off with it, they are so inspired to be in these will activities. It's of tremendous interest and comfort to the children that there is order in the world. This is strengthening for the life sense.

2.   Holding a generally positive, loving mood. This, of course, nourishes the child's sense of well-being. One year, I was fortunate to have four practicum students who came all at different times. The children welcomed these students and had various reactions to their presence in the classroom. Because of the children's reactions, I noticed that one student stood out. She was full of peace, radiating interest, and so happy to be with the children. The children were drawn to her like flies to honey. She embodied the qualities of warmth and love and joy, all of which are nourishing to the life sense.

3.   Beauty in the environment. Creating a clean, tidy and aesthetically beautiful space helps the children feel at home.

4.   Toys that are open-ended support the life sense. These help the children feel confident in their own ability to transform situations. Traditional wooden toys with movable parts are living examples of the creative ability to bring order and life-giving properties to the children. The children's cheeks turn visibly pink when playing with these toys.

5.   Some children, when building their bodies, are very sensitive to off-gassing, chemical substances, detergents, and the like. Even some of the strong essential oils we love to use can be almost painful to the children. We can protect the children by our own consciousness around these things.

6.   Regular rhythms that make sense for the children. Sometimes these rhythms can vary slightly to meet the shifting needs of the children. For instance, as the children are readying for transition into the grade school, some teachers have observed that the older children need some time together on their own. I have worked this into our regular program because, required by law, our program has a longer day. This means that the parents get their errands done before coming to pick up their children. I have specifically asked my parents to take their children directly home after school, if at all possible. This is easier for them to do when the children are with us longer. Surprisingly, the consequence of a longer kindergarten day has been that the vitality of the children is more robust and their sense of well-being tends to be more consistent.

Later in the year, in January or so, the six-year-olds do need something different. I don't see that this is a need for structured activity, but rather a need for the new capacities arising out of the six-year change to be met. I make subtle changes to the routine but I do not change the order of our day. And, for the last half hour, instead of going outside again, we lengthen the morning and play traditional games. While the younger children watch or play, the older children do more complicated things that the younger children really don't want to get involved with.

At this time, when the "birth of the etheric" turns the children into little "bubbling pots," we sometimes also take up, indoors or outdoors, the children's passion for skipping [rope]. The etheric body has an affinity to and a natural tendency to pass into cosmic space and is at home there. Rudolf Steiner says, "The etheric body is not subject to gravity—on the contrary—it is always trying to get away. Its tendency is to disperse and scatter into far cosmic spaces."[21] Remember, I previously mentioned the intimate connection of the etheric body and the life sense. No wonder the older child in the kindergarten takes such joy in skipping when the birth of the etheric is underway.

7. Children want to hear that this world they have incarnated into is safe. They want to have people around them saying, "Yes, this is a good place"; "Yes, you can test your strength in this safe place and I will protect you." We can still carry this nourishing attitude for the child's life sense while, at the same time, providing the protection of reasonable boundaries. Sometimes I think we spend too much time saying "no" for the wrong reasons. We can set healthy limits and still give the children the opportunity to challenge their strength and take reasonable risks. For example, in the child-devised wagon ride below, when the children are riding on the chairs within the wagon, it is perfectly safe as long as the children remain sitting and those pushing use their "walking feet."

In closing, what a privilege we have, as educators, to be in this supportive role, along with other mighty beings, of carefully nurturing this emerging sense of well-being in the young child. If we regard this task rightly and accept this partnership with all its graces, it can bring life-giving forces to the children as well as ourselves and others.

NOTES

1. Karl König, *A Living Physiology* (Bolton Village, UK: Camphill Books, 2006), pp. 189–93.

2. See generally Rudolf Steiner, *A Psychology of Body, Soul, and Spirit* (Great Barrington, Massachusetts: Steiner Books, 1999), originally translated and published as *The Wisdom of Man, of the Soul and of the Spirit* (New York: Anthroposophic Press, 1971).

3. See, e.g., Rudolf Steiner, *Spiritual Science as a Foundation for Social Forms* (London: Rudolf Steiner Press, 1986; Great Barrington, Massachusetts: Steiner Books, 1986).

4. Ibid.

5. Willi Aeppli, *The Care and Development of the Human Senses* (Edinburgh, UK: Floris Books, 2013), pp. 11-12.

6. König, *A Living Physiology*, pp. 188–89.

7. Henning Köhler, *Working with Anxious, Nervous, and Depressed Children* (Chatham, New York: AWSNA, 1995), p. 24-25.

8. Rudolf Steiner, *Anthroposophy—A Fragment* (Hudson, New York: Anthroposophic Press, 1996), and Rudolf Steiner, *A Psychology of Body, Soul, & Spirit* (Hudson, NY: Anthroposophic Press, 1999), pp. 20–21.

9. Ibid.

10. Rudolf Steiner, *Education as a Force for Social Change* (Hudson, New York: Anthroposophic Press, 1997), pp. 56–57.

11. Köhler, *Working with Anxious, Nervous and Depressed Children*.

12. König, *A Living Physiology*.

13. Rudolf Steiner, *The Boundaries of Natural Science* (New York: Anthroposophic Press, 1983).

14. Ruth Ker, Editor, *From Kindergarten into the Grades,* (Chestnut Ridge, New York: Waldorf Early Childhood Association of North America, 2014).

15. Rudolf Steiner, *The Essentials of Education* (Great Barrington, Massachusetts: Anthroposophic Press, 1997).

16. Ibid. at 70.

17. "We sat on flat stones and slid down the face of the large rocks. We did this until our backsides were so sore we could hardly sit down." Nelson Mandela, *The Long Walk to Freedom* (New York: Holt, Rinehart and Winston, 2000), pp. 9-10.

18. No direct transcription of Mandela's address exists, but this account is in keeping with Mandela's expressed thoughts about children and society at the time, for example, "The true character of a society is revealed in how it treats its children," 27 September, 1997, collected in "Nelson Mandela quotes about children" at *Nelson Mandela Children's Fund*, ***www.nelsonmandelachildrensfund.com/news/mandela-quotes-about-children***.

19. See, e.g., Jeff Smoth, R.N., "Earthly Nutrition, Cosmic Nutrition, and External Nursing Therapies" at AnthroMed Library, ***www.anthromed.org/Article.aspx?artpk=320***.

20. Gordon Neufeld, *Hold On to Your Kids: Why Parents Need to Matter More than Peers* (Toronto, Ontario, Candada: Vintage Canada, 2013), p. 222.

21. Rudolf Steiner, *The Roots of Education* (Hudson, New York: Anthroposophic Press, 1997), pp. 38–39.

3. Enlivening the Life Forces: Lessons from "The Donkey"

Patricia Rubano

February 9, 2014

P*atricia enters to applause and laughter—wearing a donkey tail and donkey ears.**

There's a lot of trust going on that Susan has allowed me to come up here. I might just make an ass of myself.

Her headgear falls off.

They don't make these things like they used to! My husband accommodated me last night when I said that I needed some donkey ears. A short time later—a winter hat, some paper ears, a dangling rope behind and, presto! I'm an ass!

I definitely wanted to bring the donkey along this morning after the eurythmy performance last night. It so happens that in the Biography and Social Art course, that same fairy tale informs us about life. I seem to have had an affinity for donkeys throughout my life, with Eeyore being one of my favorites. "Life is soo hard." What melancholic would not love Eeyore?

But Eeyore is not the only character living in this skin with me. I have the spoiled girl from the puppet show in me, too. "You don't

---

*Editor's notes on activity during the lecture will appear throughout.

know how hard my life is! It's so cold here! I'm used to the warmth!" And yet someone asked *me* to talk to you about enlivening the life forces? I'm still working on it! I go to school and all the parents there think that I'm wonderful and I'm so great. They put me up on that pedestal, you know? But go ask the people at home about the tired, grumpy, irritable me that they live with.

So this question of the life forces is a life's work and is ongoing. I was not sure what I would say about it because I'm sure you have been to some of the workshops covering all those things we already know—and need to be reminded of. We need to exercise and paint and dance and play—to do the things that rejuvenate us. And we do need that. Yesterday, Ruth was showing us all kinds of earthly, material things that the world around us is busy telling us that we need to take advantage of. And then there is the ever-flowing fount that Susan Weber referred to that I hope will be touched on today.

The bad news is, growth is hard work. Darn it! But the seven-year phases of development do not stop at twenty-one. A lot of you are in your thirties and forties and I remember being at those stages. It's hard! But I think the way the Asian cultures speak of life in three stages captures something quite well. The first twenty years is to learn. The middle twenty years is to fight, though I prefer the word "struggle." And the last twenty years—and these are often no longer the last years, to be sure—are to grow wise. Being in one's thirties and forties is the perfect time to take up, if you haven't already, some inner work. *Start Now*[1] is a book containing spiritual exercises given by Rudolf Steiner. Or Michael Lipson's book, *Stairway of Surprise*,[2] is a good one for the six basic exercises. To look in, to "know thyself," is vital for anyone working with children. Choosing practices that are right for you can support your own continued growth and development.

We can also start taking up other aspects of the work of becoming human for ourselves. We are always looking out for the children and the development of their lower senses. But we cannot stop with the study of child development. We must carry the picture of human development over a whole lifetime. And we cannot stop with the lower senses, which form the foundation for the future, but must take up for ourselves the development of the higher senses.

So, I wanted to bring the donkey and Rudolf Steiner along today to help me speak to some of this. I think most of you were present at the eurythmy performance of the Grimm's fairy tale, "The Donkey," last night or perhaps you are at least familiar with the story. It has become a favorite of mine and I will bring us through it this morning. At the beginning of the story we meet a king and queen who have no child. What a picture of a future that is in danger we have right there because, of course, a child is the future. Then a child comes, but the queen cannot see beyond the donkey skin. Fortunately, the king can. And this activity of learning to see beyond, that we need to take up and learn to do, is right there in the fairy tale.

I recently looked at the beginning of many fairy tales. I was looking for something else, but what I *actually* found was over and over how they start: "Once there was a little girl whose father and mother had died and she no longer had a room to live in or any possessions." Or, "There was a serving maid who went on a journey with her family. Some robbers stopped them and killed all of the family except her." The fairy tales immediately tell us that life is not easy. They tell us of trials, and they also tell us of helpers. Rudolf Steiner says that we are birthing something new into the world at this point in evolution. We are living at the time of the birth and development of the Consciousness Soul. Most of us here are women, and we know about labor pains and what it takes to bring new life into the world. Rudolf Steiner tells us that this life journey is hard and that it must be so. This new faculty of consciousness cannot come to birth without struggle and without rubbing up against one another.

The fairy tales also tell us, as Rudolf Steiner observes, that we have to break the enchantment. We have to break the spell. And one of the spells we have to break is this notion that life is supposed to be easy.

If we "do it right," it is going to be smooth and easy. Growing up in a church, I think I learned that, if I do it right and if I am good and pious like the little girl in the story, it will be smooth. I will be blessed and my prayers will be answered. Then that scenario did not work so well for me, so I found the Eastern traditions and there was a lot that spoke to me deeply. But there was also the notion of enlightenment. So I wanted to be enlightened. I thought this was a static state that I could get to. I wanted to get there. And then it was all going to be okay. But the real teaching for enlightenment is, "Before enlightenment, chop wood, carry water. After enlightenment, chop wood, carry water." That is really what I am here to tell you.

Have you seen the light in someone's eyes, like Janene Ping when she said, "I love a good story!"—the light in Ruth's eyes when she was sharing with us about the mud and sand and all the working in the garden? We all love a story, but what makes a good story? It is all the characters in it and all the drama and tension and excitement. We have to remember that *all* those characters in the story—any story—are in each one of us. All of the characters are me.

I have that spoiled little girl in me and I also have the good little girl in me who takes care of her mother, who takes care of the plants. And I think that this is another enchantment, this view that I am I and you are you. And we are enclosed in these singular, individual donkey-skin bodies. St. Francis referred to his body as Brother Ass. That is the one who carries me through life, but is this body that carries me through life who I really am? What part do all these other parts within and the people outside have to do with "who I am"?

How do I develop those higher senses that let me come into a real sense of the ego of the other? What is it to be a human being? To "know thyself"? What is this human becoming?

Signe Schaefer was the founder of the Biography and Social Arts Program here at Sunbridge. And she has written a book, *Why on Earth? Biography and the Practice of Human Becoming.*[3]

At some point Steiner essentially says that it is impossible to really *be* a human being now. But it is always possible to step into the *becoming*.

So how do we do this? How do we step into this? As I have already said, we cannot stop with the lower senses. We cannot stop with child development alone. We have to ask ourselves the questions that the fairy tale asks. Can we see behind? Can we see beyond? Can we hear not what is said but what is meant—the thought behind the words? Can we follow the thoughts of another? These questions have to do with the higher senses.

I can reflect back to when I first heard of the twelve senses and studied them. I tried so long to memorize what they were and had to keep going back to the book, so I will remind you. These lower senses are the ones that tell us about ourselves—the senses of touch, of life, self-movement, and the sense of balance. Then we go into the middle senses, and these tell us about the interweaving of self and world. These are the senses of smell, taste, sight, and warmth. But the higher senses are the ones that tell us about the other person. These are the senses of hearing, of the spoken word, the sense of concept, and the sense of the ego of the other. And this life sense we have been talking about and tending to needs to form the basis and evolve into this sense of concept, the sense of thought. Can I follow the thoughts of another? And what this requires of me is to lay down my own thoughts for a time and be able to follow along with the thoughts of another. But to do that, I have to strengthen my own "I."

There are two directions we can travel to work on this and ideally we will travel both—one moves inward and the other moves outward—both in service to our task, which as I understand it is to learn to love out of freedom.

What can phases of human development tell us about this?

How many here were children?

All raise their hands.

Good—I thought so! So, we have all had the benefit of the hierarchies to carry us in our childhood development—a "natural" development carries us. We learn to walk, talk, and think by the grace of the gods, not by being taught. And as adults, Steiner suggests that much of what we need to do is to get out of the way so the child can develop. We know this and see it and trust it. Whereas the rest of the world is saying, "Teach them. Teach them," we are saying, "Remove the obstacles, create the right environment, be worthy of imitation and the children will develop." It is in the nature of the children to learn from everything around them.

We are carried, as I said, to a certain point, then gradually engage ever more consciously in our own learning. But eventually comes the time where Steiner tells us that "natural" development comes to an end and it is truly up to us to take up self-development for ourselves—or not. Somewhere in our late twenties or early thirties we notice that a certain invisible support and the "natural" talents we had begin to fade if we do not now bring something new out of ourselves and make them our own. Between twenty-eight and thirty there is often an inner crisis of sorts.

I hope that you have all at least heard of the six basic exercises and have some familiarity with them. Many teachers have told me that they learned of these in teacher training but could not really relate to them or tried them but then could not sustain them. I will say personally that I have tried them and laid them down and tried them and laid them down. But the older I get and the more I work with them, the more dear they are to my heart. They are meant to help us strengthen and gain a mastery over our thinking, feeling, and willing. I will briefly review them now.

Rudolf Steiner gave these exercises as a necessary strengthening to prepare for meditation, but I think we could say they are a necessary companion for life in the twenty-first century. He gives us a concentration exercise to do for only five minutes a day. The objective is to keep my mind focused on one thing for five minutes, something mundane like a paper clip. In doing this, I find a strengthening happening in the realm of thoughts.

Next is the one that I fail at consistently even to this day. This is the will exercise. To do something for no other reason than that you have decided to do it. I do not think of myself as a weak-willed person, but this exercise made me realize that most of what I do is motivated by or done on behalf of others. To consistently do something simply because I decide to do it is hard.

Then in the realm of feeling is the goal of developing equanimity by attending to feelings but expressing them only as you choose to. Then come practices for positivity and open-mindedness. And the sixth weaves them all together. So this is just an example of the myriad ways of inner work that Steiner gives. Many other exercises are out there that are so valuable—if we practice.

I really appreciate that there are so many other spiritual teachers of our day who are saying essentially the same things we hear from Rudolf Steiner—and even brain research supports so much of what we are doing. For me, that validates these thoughts I have been living with for years. If others are saying similar things in different words, that to me says, "Yes, consciousness is evolving." One does not have to be an anthroposophist to wake up to the fact that there is more than this material world, and this acknowledgment is happening all around.

There are certain things at certain moments that we need to hear. When I was in my thirties and was dealing with chronic fatigue, I felt like a veil was in front of me. I just couldn't make my way through it to the people and the world around me in the midst of that stage of life with all its responsibilities and stresses. And I think Dr. Michaela Glöckler gave a lecture where she spoke about cultivating interest. Since then I have seen how often the importance of this quality of interest streams out of so much that Steiner says. Thich Nhat Hanh also says that "inter-est"—to inter-be—is the ability to stream into the other. This has been a real key for me. Steiner's work and that of Georg Kühlewind describe that when the child's etheric forces are freed from growth as their primary task, then the child can begin to think. Forces continue to be freed. As we get older and our life forces decline in the body, these forces are freed for our use in other ways. These freed forces Kühlewind speaks of as freed forces of attention. These may be used consciously or they may become masterless forces being drawn by whatever harnesses them. It is an aspect of our freedom that we can choose where to put our attention.

We each have our particular interests—puppetry, singing, and so on—that we naturally gravitate toward and take joy in. I always thought that interest is something that just sort of happens to us and that we had little control over. It is true that we are born with particular gifts and inclinations, but it was a revelation for me to consider that we can choose what to be interested in! The secret is that I can choose where to put my attention.

I have made a discovery through doing a perception exercise with other people. We observe a stone and then inwardly picture it as accurately as possible, back and forth a few times. Then we look in a different way—one that asks the stone to "reveal thyself," back and forth a few times. What I have found is that everyone falls in love with their stone and a certain progression occurs through this practice of attention. I describe it in this way: Wherever I put my attention, interest arises. Wherever interest arises, I can actually come to an understanding. Where there is understanding, I tend to fall in love. So this freedom of what we do with our attention actually potentially leads to love. This was so strong for me because I thought, If we can fall in love with a stone simply through consciously placing our attention there, what would be possible if we did that with one another? This whole process makes me think of a child study—to practice objective observation without analyzing and also ask inwardly and reverently for the child to "reveal thyself."

There is a short quotation from John Tarrant, a Zen teacher. He says: "Attention is the most basic form of love. Through it, we bless and are blessed."[4]

What drains our life forces? For me it is feeling disconnected, it is feeling separated. It is feeling enclosed in my own little shell here, my own little world. Steiner says that this is the way of the world right now. That is what is "normal." We are developing the Consciousness Soul, and that means that the antisocial forces are stronger than the social forces. To be conscious of something, to be able to see it, we have to be apart from it. We no longer easily sense our way into the other. Because of this, we walk around enclosed in our own "habit" like hermits who do not even see each other. We are solitary beings.

One of the two directions spoken of earlier is this inner work. I work with my own "I" to strengthen my faculties of thinking, feeling, and willing. And the other direction is to put our attention out into the world. Steiner says in many different ways—to find the world, look into yourself. To find yourself, look into the world. And we can do this with the natural world, as in the exercise of concentrating upon and picturing the stone. We observe it and find ourselves falling in love with it. Or a tree. Steiner suggests that this is a good way to come into touch with the elementals. A practice done in many training courses, including the biography course, is to follow something in the natural world through the course of a whole year, thus helping ourselves learn to observe, to see the processes of growth and development that are present in any life form.

Where else can we practice this? As mentioned, we do this with child study and we learn a lot about development. I question whether many of us think to do this in the adult sphere. It behooves us to do our own biography work to look at our own life and see what has formed us. A lot of people may think that biography work is just navel-gazing and that psychology is just an inner turning. What I am trying to say here is that biography work can be an outer turning also, because we are dealing with an enchantment by which we think we have formed our own lives. Have you ever thought much about the fact that most people have little to no memory of the first three years of life or more? We are here on earth and living a life, but someone else actually holds the memory of that time for you! That is an amazing thought to me—that someone else holds a part of my life for me. And whenever we look back on our lives, it is filled with all the different characters in the story. We find all the people who have helped us to become who we are—the prince and princess, the wicked witch, and the troll. They are all there. They are there outside of us and they are also there inside us. What better way to wake up to them than, in our Waldorf way, through a fairy tale with a little biography work alongside?

In biography work, there are infinite entry points into exploring our lives. There are temperaments, soul types, and the seven-year phases themselves, to name a few. But a fairy tale is a wonderful way to enter in. (Please note that anything I say about this fairy tale should be taken as a suggestion—with a question mark. We cannot pin down fairy tales. If we do, it is like pinning an insect on the display board. It is dead. We want to ask "I wonder? Perhaps it means this.") For our own little practice right now, here are some questions and thoughts to ponder:

At the beginning of "The Donkey," there is a queen who cannot see beyond the donkey skin. She has wept night and day, lamenting her barrenness and thus has not slept—has not entered into the night-time, spiritual world. She is a wreck, and can see only the physical, outer appearance. Is this why she cannot see the ego of the other? She says that she would rather have had no child than to have a donkey. If the queen is a picture of the feminine, the soul, then we must consider what condition the feminine, the soul of the human being has come to. She is the old queen and has been awake to the material world too long. She does not see clearly and is awash in emotion. But it is clear that the king, the spirit in each of us, can still see the true nature of the child—or at least accept that the child is as God has chosen to create it. He sees the donkey as his child, his heir, and will have him treated as such.

In our own lives, there have been people who could see and recognize us and there have been people who could not. For yourself, take a moment to remember and inwardly thank a couple of the people who saw you. Individually, we may also be able to say thank you even to those who did not see us because something happened out of that, too.

Patricia pauses silently for a moment; the audience follows suit.

Now, on with our little donkey tale! It is possible to see four trials in this fairy tale; there are always trials in a fairy tale. The first we could consider an earth trial. Our little donkey has hooves, but he wants to play the lyre; he wants to master the physical form he has in order to play and create music. Because he is "persevering and industrious," and no excuses can stop him, he transforms his hooves to play as "well as the master himself." Relating this to our own lives, we can ask ourselves what we have taken up to develop because we were drawn to something, but it took hard work. The puppet show we saw was a lot of work to stage and perform, but did you see how the puppeteers loved their work? What is something that we each have had to work at? Turn to your neighbor and share for just a few minutes.

The auditorium erupts into vibrant sharing.

Our donkey masters the earthly form he has been given. But at a certain moment he is melancholy and goes out walking. He sees his donkey's form reflected in a well—could we see this as a water trial? He is so shocked that this sends him on a journey. Has there been a time in your life when you received a reflection that was rather shocking? Yes? This can take many different forms. I can share an experience of working with a particular assistant one year. This person had been hired when I was away, so we had never met in person. I am ultimately grateful for this encounter because it came at a time when I was asking to really see myself as others see me—and I had learned by then, as a Native American teacher put it, to pray for things to come in good and gentle ways. It was not an easy relationship and this was new for me. One good thing was that we could face one another and admit that our encounters were not easy. But we realized that we had something to do with each other and we shared a language that let us speak about an element of karma that we felt was at work. The assistant told me that I reminded her of a sister whom she had not spoken to in years. She lambasted me one day just before class and said that I never told her anything she was doing well—I only told her things that she was doing wrong. Fortunately, I had had enough experience in my life by then to know that I work pretty well with people and that this was an overstatement, at least. I could let go of the part that felt like it was her own reactivity, but I had to try to understand her experience and find what part did belong to me.

It was painful to realize that I could recognize this criticism from my husband about how I was at home. I can always see how something could be done differently, or better—and I point it out. When I was growing up, my father never told us that we did something right or well—that was just to be expected. If you did not do something right, then that was what you heard about from my two perfectionist parents. So I could trace this back and see how I had inherited this and how it lived on in me. That was a shocking reflection because I recognized something unpleasant about myself that sent me on an inner journey to learn to share my appreciation of others, and I still continue to work at this.

Sometimes it is an outer journey. A friend had a high school teacher who told him that he could never make it in college. I don't recall whether the friend had thought to go on to college or not, but the result of this teacher's comment or "reflection" was that he took it as a challenge to show that he could make it. He went to college and later ended up as a Waldorf teacher. So we can ponder this, too. Where have we received reflections—from a child, parent, colleague—that have sent us on a journey? Where have these journeys taken you? What changes occurred? While I am posing these questions for you to consider for yourself right now, if you wanted to do this in a way that supports social understanding and connection, you could do this within your faculties and share about your journeys. Small sharings go a long way.

Generally, we only do this kind of thing when we have a natural sympathy or affinity for someone, so we become friends and we share some of our life stories. But this is the same thing as "interest happening to us." This sharing of stories can be life changing and we can *choose* to do it. We can even choose to do it with people with whom we do not have a natural affinity. And something happens; something transforms in the doing. An early childhood faculty, for example, could take any fairy tale and explore it in this way. Working with it will deepen your understanding of the fairy tale and also of your own life and of one another.

Returning to the story. The donkey takes with him on his journey "one faithful companion." The story does not identify this companion—is it his lute? His angel? His true self? This is one of the mysteries in the story, but we do know that he has his lute. I think of this next part as the air trial.

He is on the journey and he decides, "Here we shall stay." This ass is very decisive and we can find a lot of will in this story. He comes to this kingdom where an old king has a beautiful daughter, but the gate does not open when he calls, "A guest is without—open that he may enter." This is not sufficient, so he sits down and begins to play—I imagine that he brings a heavenly music, the music of the spheres. He has overcome his hooves to become a master musician; he has seen his true form in the water and gone on a journey and now the air carries the truth and essence of his being to the gatekeeper. The gatekeeper, however, cannot believe his eyes—a much more outward directed sense—but he does hear, which is already one of the higher senses. He tells the king what he has heard, the door is opened and our little ass enters a new kingdom.

Maybe there is a special gift each of us has that has opened doors for us. Maybe there have been moments when we just knew that there was something we had to do, and that meant entering a new realm. Something new is required to cross that threshold, and our donkey has developed something on his journey. He will not sit with the servants or the soldiers. "I am no common stable ass. I am a noble one. I will sit by the king." He has developed will, but there is still something lacking. The king asks, "How does my daughter please you?" He knows immediately, "I like her above measure." One of my teachers pointed out that this phrase may hold a hint about this new realm we have entered. We are above the quantifiable world. This is a world beyond measure—a world of qualities.

To sit beside her is exactly what he is wishing for. He behaves "daintily and cleanly" and it seems that he is well suited to be in this kingdom, but eventually he comes before the king looking sad. He still is in need of the Parzival question. He needs something, some higher part of himself to draw out his deepest need and desire. And the king asks him, "What ails you? I wish I did know what would make you content." And then then there is a series of tests. "Do you want gold?" "Do you want jewels and rich dress?" "Do you want half of my kingdom?" The donkey answers no to each of these offers. Though he does not seem to know it himself yet, he is looking for something else; "I want my soul. I want the other half of myself." In this story, the trials are not necessarily outward as in a battle or task, but are more inward as we are told that the donkey is despondent and wants to go home. "What good does all of this do me?" Have we ever ourselves felt that way? Sometimes I think, "I have meditated for all this long time, gone to how many workshops, but what good does it do me? I still have this donkey skin on! I don't fit—I'm not enough."

The donkey has persevered and been industrious, he has recognized his imperfect form and can sound his true tone. He has a strong will. He has gone through all these other trials, but he still needs and we need someone to ask us, "What ails thee?"

The longing to be seen and heard in our full reality has arisen in every human soul since the beginning of the twentieth century and is growing increasingly urgent.

We long to be seen and heard inside our donkey skins. We can feel that. This longing was not there in the same way in my parents and certainly not in my grandparents. That is part of the Consciousness Soul times we live in. We have work to do here, so we need each other. We need someone to see us and to hear us into our full reality.

So the king does see or at least senses and he asks, "Do you want my pretty daughter to be your wife?" And the donkey immediately knows and answers, "Oh yes, that is exactly what I have been wishing for." And so the wedding takes place.

The princess in this story says little, but I love the line when the father asks her in the morning after her wedding night, "But surely you are sad that you have not got a proper man for your husband?" and she answers, "Oh no, dear father, I love him as well as if he were the handsomest in the world and I will keep him as long as I live!" I like to think that this is the soul that loves unconditionally and provides the safety to reveal oneself wholly and fully. The one with whom we can enter the holy of holies and sense the "I" of the other. Is that not what we are all longing for?

So the donkey has been seen in his full reality, but the "coming out" is not easy. There remains one more trial to undergo. And it requires the king—the masculine, the spirit—to do it. After he has learned that at night a handsome prince steps out of the donkey skin and reveals himself to the princess, he takes the donkey's skin and burns it! Some people are angry about this part of the story—I have come to really appreciate that king in his role as helper and witness. He stays awake all night and watches—he does not desert the young prince, but "wants to see how the robbed man will behave." Who is the king, really? Who stands watch as we struggle through our own karma?

Most of us know the picture that Steiner gives of that other part of us that goes along with us in life. This is the one who, while we are walking along the street, runs ahead, climbs to the roof and loosens the brick that will fall on us. To get more insight into one's eternal being, one should look at the events and people in life that have been the most difficult. We identify with the pleasant event, but the difficult events are more 'me' than that which goes easily. I have, with real intention, loosened that brick to fall on my head. This "second man" in "me" just may be the one at work in these matters of destiny. Sometimes it looks like someone else did something, or sometimes it just looks like a random life event. This could be an illness, a loss, or an accident. Whatever vehicle it comes through, it just might be that I myself have intended it.

What can we make of this burning of the skin? What is the effect of this deed? When we work with this story in the Biography and Social Art course, we explore this question. Consider for yourselves what skins have been burned in your life? Those times that were not necessarily comfortable or easy. Maybe someone encouraged, nudged or even pushed you to do something you didn't feel ready for…maybe there was a sudden change or a great loss that left you feeling vulnerable and naked…what part of yourself was then revealed or even developed as a result?

If there was time, we could all share, but since there is not, I will share one of mine with you.

I can tell you that I felt very nervous when Susan Howard asked me to speak at this conference. It would have been easy to say, "Thanks, but no thanks." But I was able to recognize a progression in my own life and a model of development through someone else that allowed me to take a deep breath and say, "Okay."

As a new teacher here at Green Meadow, I found it intimidating just to hold a parent meeting, but I got used to it. Then I could speak before a larger group of parents at an all-school meeting. Then I began to work with adults and groups more often. I became more comfortable and not only that, but I watched Joan Almon go from being "just another Waldorf early childhood teacher" to become a dynamic speaker at conferences like this. So, although each new step was a challenge and sometimes a trial and I would never have considered it on my own, someone else saw a capacity in me and nudged. And though it felt like a big risk—"What if I make an ass of myself?"—I accepted. Now, that's not a big one, but I can tell you that

I still feel quite vulnerable, a bit like standing here naked before you and that's why it helped to put on that donkey disguise!

The fairy tale itself is more dramatic than my example, but through the burning of the skin, the donkey's true self is revealed to all. When he accepts the invitation to stay there in his true form, he inherits the kingdom. He inherits not only one kingdom but two. This is a special story, for he inherits both heaven and earth! This may tell of a time only very far in the future, but isn't this what we are going for? We cannot live with only one. We want and need both.

Why should we go through all of this? I will acknowledge again that this life path is hard work, but I want to also call up the picture of young children. All we have to do is look to them. What do they have to do to learn to walk? How many times do they fall? We are trying to urge parents to allow the children this natural struggle so that they can grow strong in themselves. We, too, need the struggle to grow strong and maybe we can even try to learn to love the struggle—our own and those of others—as a natural part of development. We need each other to share the struggle or at least to play witness to one another. And we need to celebrate the achievements and enjoy the results, like the puppet shows and the beautiful environments we create and the joy we engender in the children. Is there anything more wonderful than the beaming of a child when they break through and achieve a new skill or capacity? Let us be that with and for one another!

In Steiner's words: "To contemplate the destinies of human beings with reverence and awe, that is something our times demand of us."[5] We can do this by reading biographies, but what if we did this for the people closest to hand?

Even stronger is Steiner's emphasis on the importance of an understanding of destiny. Humanity will not be able to survive unless it takes the reality of destiny into its consciousness.[6]

We are living in a depressed world. The visions of the future, even for the children, are fuzzy and often bleak. Like the beginning of this fairy tale, the future is in danger. But the fairy tales also tell us that if we meet the trials with a pure and simple heart, there is a marriage at the end and a new king and queen will inherit the kingdom. We do have a destiny and there is somewhere that we are going. If we learn to work with one another in community with this knowledge, we are building invisible temples together. It is our karmic ties that connect us so that we may build the mystery temples of today. We need each other. As Rudolf Steiner wrote, "The things done here on earth through love, friendship and the intimate understanding of one another; these are the building stones of temples being erected in the regions of spirit. For those convinced of this truth, it should be an uplifting feeling to know that the ties binding soul to soul are the basis for eternal being."[7]

It is true that the natural world revives us, but to have a true encounter with another human being enlivens us. We are all experts at meetings! How many meetings do we sit in? But do we consider that every meeting we sit in holds the potential to meet and encounter one another? If I am practicing control of thought, then maybe that can be a chance to keep my thought on what the other is actually saying, not what I am going to do when I go home or what I will say next. If I am practicing will, I can attend to what I am doing in my limbs. Do I cross my arms? Turn away? Roll my eyes? These are all expressions of my will as it lives unconsciously in my body; in my movement. I can work on these things. And obviously I can practice equanimity when that person over there is saying *that* again! Positivity that we will win through to a unified vision in the end—that even the obstacles have a role to play and will add something.

I know well that there is always plenty of opportunity to practice open-mindedness in a school community. And this requires letting go of a lot of what I think and hold dear—hard work indeed! We have to practice these things in community. And when we do, people become more real to us—they become more three-dimensional. This rubbing up against one another is actually what Steiner says will wake us up to karma.

We believe that we are with this group of people for a reason, that our karma has brought us together. But until we wake up to who they are in a true, three-dimensional, full-bodied way, we cannot discover what we might have to do with each other. When we direct our attention toward these others we become more and more interested and if we are open to them, we will gain new understanding. When we truly understand one another, the inclination to criticize and blame falls away and genuine compassion and empathy arise.

I will let these gray donkey hairs of mine speak and say that once upon a time, I thought this earth was not such a great place to be and I resisted and resented being here. Now, many years and much hard work later, I love my colleagues, even the difficult ones. I love the parents, even the difficult ones, because when I see them, I see what stands behind them as a whole life story. I seldom know the details, or what their childhood was like, but when you work with parent-child classes, you do get to hear some of that just in the sharing, especially when you get to do some study time with the parents alone. All the images from the many life stories I have been privileged to receive through so many people have awakened in me a genuine feeling of karma over time. With these gray and white hairs, I can actually speak about karma now. When I was younger I believed it but could not talk about it because it wasn't real for me. But it is real now. When I enter into any group, there stands the question of what have we to do with each other and I believe I have learned to see some of it playing out.

We do have something to do with each other. We have something to offer each other. Over time, this illusion that I am me and you are you can begin to dissolve and the hold of our antisocial egotistical orientation begins to lessen.

Children are allowed to be egotistical and selfish—because their "self" is still the whole world. They need to be egotistical as young children so that in old age they can give blessing because they no longer need to be egotistical. Life is a process of coming into our

73

individuality, our "I," and then, when it is strongly established, to be able to step aside a little bit. Entering into the thoughts of another requires me to "lay down my own life for another"—to lay down my cherished opinions and beliefs. Kühlewind says something like that and it opened a door for me. I had always thought that "laying down one's life" was only about physically dying, but I now see how I have to die to myself in order to make room for another. The more I have managed to lay aside my world conception and my opinions for a time, to try to see what the other sees, what a relief I have found it to be! I am lighter. To enter into the ideas and opinions of another is one path to the Christ, according to Steiner. There are other ways, but this is one.

When we feel a connection, we find meaning. When we read a book, watch a movie, hear a story, we begin to see the threads that stand behind the events. We should learn to do this for one another. The thread is not so easily seen in our own lives. It is so easy to look at someone else's life and say, "I can see why that keeps happening to her over and over. It's so obvious!" Can I look at my own life in the same way? Yes, we can begin to see the threads and the meaning in our own lives as we learn to bring objectivity to our own lives as we share pieces with others—as we see the archetype of human development that stands behind our own unique and individual life. As I listen to the stories of others, I begin to experience that I am you and you are me. The veil separating us begins to grow thinner. I am living this particular life in this unique way, but the "I" is not those details. Rather, that "I" is the essential core of my being that is moving through these experiences. The amazing thing is that as I strengthen this sense of my "I," it becomes more possible for me to lay it aside. The more I share my life story, the less attached I am to it; the less I feel it is "mine" and the more it is "a" life being lived. The more I lay down my life for another, the more I can truly see myself. And the more comfortable and at peace I feel with who I am, the happier my life sense is, but not in a physical way. The more my life sense is at ease, the more I can enter into the thoughts and make space for the ego of the other. The opposite of this on the physical level is when we are ill, when our life sense is off and we feel raw and don't want to be touched, we cannot think for ourselves or follow the thoughts of another. These are the ways that I can make some links for myself between the lower and the higher senses. Being in touch with my body and at ease in my life sense may be the key to the transformation—the turning inside out—of the lower senses of touch and life to become the sense of concept that can follow the thoughts of another and the sense of the "I" of the other, that can enter into that holy space—or let it enter me.

I fully believe that everyone longs to be seen and heard in their full reality. But it has occurred to me that if we are all waiting for someone else to see and understand us, who is doing the seeing, who is doing the hearing, who is doing the understanding? We have to take turns for each other. This is a real social deed for the times we live in; to offer our attention and our warmth of interest to another. And this is what will give birth to the new faculty that wants to come into being—this Consciousness Soul—that will ultimately lead us beyond our own little "I."

I realize that this little thing that I call "I" is the same "I" that the other is carrying around inside their skin. I am just manifesting it in this way right now and you in your way, but we can meet somewhere up higher where this shared "I" is.

Once upon a time there was a little girl who was born into a world where a beast was growing larger and larger. But the little girl wanted to change the world and to protect the children. So she took on the disguise of a kindergarten teacher—or sometimes a donkey—and she found that by changing herself, she changed the world. And by changing the world, she changed herself. We need to care for the children; we need to care for each other. Thank you for caring.

NOTES

1. Rudolf Steiner, *Start Now!: A Book of Soul and Spiritual Exercises* (Great Barrington, Massachusetts: SteinerBooks, 2004).

2. Michael Lipson, *Stairway of Surprise: Six Steps to a Creative Life* (Anthroposophic Press, 2002).

3. Signe Eklund Schaefer, *Why on Earth?: Biography and the Practice of Human Becoming* (Great Barrington, Massachusetts: SteinerBooks, 2013).

4. Susan Piver, *The Wisdom of a Broken Heart* (New York: Atria Paperback, 2010), page 50. For further information about John Tarrant, see **www.pacificzen.org/teachers/john-tarrant** and **tarrantworks.com/about**.

5. Rudolf Steiner, *Karmic Relationships: Esoteric Studies, Volume 2* (Forest Row, UK: Rudolf Steiner Press, 2004) page 208.

6. See, e.g., Rudolf Steiner, "The Three Realms of the Dead: Life Between Death and a New Birth" in *The Reappearance of Christ in the Etheric* (Great Barrington, Massachusetts: SteinerBooks, 2003): "A true understanding of destiny is the important development that must spread over the earth. It must take hold in legislation and in the form of political parties; it must provide the very foundation of society. Anything incompatible with the spiritual evolution of humankind will simply dissolve; it will break down."

7. Rudolf Steinter, *Rosicrucian Wisdom: An Introduction* (Forest Row, UK: Rudolf Steiner Press, 2005), page 45.

4. Nurturing the Sense of Life and Well-Being

Adam Blanning, M.D.

February 6-8, 2015

Introduction

February 6, 2015

It is pretty easy, as a physician who often sees sickness, to experience the life sense of another person. If you glance at someone across the room, you can get a read on that person's life sense. When the life sense is functioning well, we take it for granted. The feeling we can have after a good meal is an experience of life sense. When we are tired, we experience a diminished life sense. We can see a disturbed life sense in children who are uneasy and restless, who need a lot of attention and direction. These needs often come forth suddenly in transition times. Circle has ended. It is time for free play and there is a problem. A similar moment can happen when we are starting to put on snow clothes. One of these children always has an argument or meltdown. This is an expression of an imbalanced, undeveloped life sense.

We can enter into what this feels like for the child with an exercise. Let us focus our vision across the room very precisely. This should be very easy for us to do. If we woke up in the morning and couldn't do this, it would be distressing. Now let go of vision and think of breathing. Take a deep breath. Take some fast breaths. This is not too bad. But maybe we haven't been thinking about breath all day long. If we woke up and had to think about our breathing, it would be a bad thing. Breathing is usually automatic. Now slow down your heart rate. Now try to speed it up a little bit—imagine that someone has jumped out from behind and scared you. There are people who do practice control of heart rate through such things as biofeedback or meditative practices that work with the breath. We can slow the heart rate through the breath.

Now increase the blood flow to your spleen. That is too hard. Contract your gall bladder. From anatomy we know that the spleen is on left, the gall bladder on the right side of the body. But we should not actually know this from personal experience. As we go on a descent from looking and seeing, to breathing, then to the pulse, we get lower down into unconscious realms that are more asleep.

Now think about doing something that really helps you to relax. Write down on your note paper what that was.

Now we can practice more thinking about the life sense. We can observe the life sense by whether we are hungry or not. Try to feel, "Am I hungry?" There are variations of this—satisfied, nauseated, or full. "Am I thirsty? Do I need to go to the bathroom?" These are all aspects of the life sense. Children who have a disturbed life sense may have trouble connecting to these body states. They do not normally sense if they are hungry and then are suddenly starving and get frantic. Or we may see a child who eats and eats without awareness of when "full" has been reached. We think that this is not healthy for them. This is an imbalance in life sense. Needing to go to the bathroom frequently is an imbalance. It is also an imbalance for the child who does not feel the need and waits and waits until it is too late and has an accident.

For yourselves as kindergarten teachers, ask yourself, "How tired am I?" Most of us all override the life sense when it comes to this question. Another aspect of imbalance is not knowing when one is tired.

Hunger, thirst, needing to go to the bathroom, and fatigue are all pathways to the life sense that let us know how we are feeling. When all these are working well, we feel well and complete. Like with the lullaby that we sang earlier today with Eleanor Winship, there is a harmony of the inner world when all systems are functioning well. This is a healthy life sense.

One way to approach how we can learn of the life sense of the child would be to ask, "How do you feel?" If the child has eaten five bowls of porridge, we could ask whether he or she is hungry. We could develop a questionnaire and ask the child to rate on a scale of one to ten, "How is your hunger, thirst, fatigue?" We could strategize this and, of course, it sounds atrocious. But we can see that there are children whose lives are very much like this. "Are you hungry? Shall we go? Are you having fun? Do you want a snack?" This is asking the child to think and analyze how he feels using the intellect, which is in a totally different realm of than the life sense.

LIFE   *TASTE*

    SELF-   *SMELL*

    MOVEMENT   *TOUCH*

             BALANCE

Diagram derived from Spiritual Science as a Foundation for Social Forms *by Rudolf Steiner (Hudson, NY: Anthroposophic Press, 1986). Discussion of these senses proceeds from right to left, beginning with TASTE and then descending in an arc through the other senses, leading ultimately to LIFE.*

How do we get to the life sense by considering what we do with a newborn baby? If she is distressed, how do we calm her? The best response is to nurse. Nursing is related to the sense of taste. This is the best route for the newborn. The baby travels directly from taste to the life sense. This is built in. It is fantastic. A newborn nurses and the world is good. She has a complete sense of well-being.

As the baby gets a little older, it can be helpful to have someone else hold the baby sometimes, like dad. Dad tries everything and then gives the baby back to mom. As soon as the child is in mom's arms and can smell the mother, the baby calms. The baby comes to mother who smells of milk. Immediately all is well.

What is the next stage? What works if one doesn't have milk and the right smell? We swaddle the baby, put a hat on her head, and hold her securely. As soon as the limbs come in and the baby feels protected, she calms. Here we deal with touch.

When babies are older, swaddling doesn't calm and satisfy any more. Then we put the baby up on the shoulder, pat, and move. The baby is being moved. Being moved engages the sense of balance (known as the vestibular system in the mainstream world).

Then at a certain point we put the baby down and the baby moves himself. The baby then goes into self-movement (proprioception in mainstream terminology).

This progression is important because all of us trace these steps on our pathway into the world. In this progression, Steiner actually starts with VISION placed above TASTE on this diagram. In *Spiritual Science as a Foundation for Social Forms,*[1] Steiner began with vision, which is an orientation point for experience of the world as the human being grows older. We go out into the world and see and touch something as a beginning point to enter this pathway to the life sense. But if we just take care of a baby, we can build this progression ourselves, beginning with taste. This ordering is different from Rudolf Steiner's other lectures, where touch is the innermost sense. Steiner says that with touch we actually feel ourselves. If I grip my piece of chalk, it is hard. If I grip my tie, it is relatively soft. I am sensing how my hand changes; the object I am touching does not change; the change occurs within myself. Taste is an outward sense. Smell is more inward. The life sense is how I feel myself in myself.

Children struggling with the life sense will go to one of the other senses as a beginning point. Every time we try to go to sleep or self-soothe, we go through this pathway of the senses. Before we go to sleep, we often move, wipe our face on the pillow, and so forth. There is lots of touching. We do this as a pathway to the life sense. Going to sleep is the greatest opportunity to practice traveling this inward pathway. We have to travel this path when we wake up and need to settle to go back to sleep. This also happens when we are in a social situation and don't know what to do. When a child with a healthy life sense is in this spot, he has an anchor. Other children who do not have this anchor go to another sensory spot on the pathway to help them get to the security provided by the life sense—bumping into someone else, moving in big ways. This can be the child who destroys circle time at the reverential moment. "They should get a a better life sense," we might wish we could say! "The parents should get them a better life sense, pronto!"

Or we can understand that the child at this moment has lost his moorings and doesn't know where to go. We live in a world out away from this inner path. This pathway has to happen in the first seven years. If it doesn't happen before the change of teeth, developing this pathway becomes a therapeutic activity. We can be so bombarded by the world that the life sense never actually develops.

We can take an example from a Waldorf school lantern walk. At a particular school the lantern walk ends at second grade. Beyond that grade, the mood gets pretty frenetic. Why? It is dark, and we are used to orienting everything by our vision. There was screaming and yelling. With vision withdrawn, children went to hearing, which is higher on the continuum of senses, as a means of orientating. Many children also began banging, crashing, and running. We can understand that when the children's vision was gone, they had to collide with something or they were totally lost—run or be lost; spin or be lost. Rather than view these as troublesome behaviors, we can see that these are signals that life sense is underdeveloped in providing an anchor so the child feels secure. Using these senses is actually very wise compensation for trying to get to the life sense.

When we see a child going crazy before nap, we can think of the disturbed life sense. We watch and if a child shows that he needs touch, we give it to him before he begins to go wild. We give strong touch, with compressions or something heavy to carry. We can ask the child to hold open a door with a heavy spring that is hard to hold open. We work to understand what the child is seeking through disrupting behaviors and provide socially healthy ways for him to get to the life sense.

Further discussion arises from a lecture attendee's question: What of a child who begins yelling at nap time? Touch has not soothed her. I would respond that there are lots of children who are unpracticed in this pathway. It is hard, so they will find ways to orient that do not involve the lower senses of self-movement, balance, and touch, but go to upper senses such as hearing. Find out how the child sleeps at home. What steps does the child take then?

There is a natural progression of the child becoming more independent in going out into the world. In his first year of life, the child holds up his head (about three months), sits independently (six months), crawls (nine months), and walks (twelve months). As he is moving into the world in motor development, there should at the same time be a reciprocal movement inward toward self-soothing. As a physician, I try to help families find a good bridging moment for the child to find the way into sleep other than nursing on the breast. When? As a doctor I experience that somewhere about six to nine months a family comes to consult. Baby is doing pretty well but mom looks exhausted. Six to nine months of interrupted sleep seems too much for the family's healthy balance. I recommend that at about four months there is nursing, a little bit of playing, and then going to sleep. If this can be worked toward before six months, it will be much easier to step forward into the time when rhythm and schedule really need to be more consistent. A newborn is living in the arc taste/smell/touch. During the time leading up to six months, we can shift the emphasis to smell/touch/ balance. There is, of course, great variation in viewpoints about nursing. Each situation is family- and culture-specific.

Here are some take-away points:

- This pathway into reaching the life sense takes a lot of practice. When we see children in distress who are acting out, consider whether they are invoking the other senses as a pathway to get to the life sense. They are not terrible little people. They are thwarted in getting to the security of the life sense and are doing what they know in order to feel good. The older the child, the more important it is for her to chart this path independently. Touch is a beautiful way to calm and feel. Giving a back scratch and massage can work well for a while. But if it works and we adults and the child become dependent on this as the gateway, it can go on for too long. A backrub of 45 minutes or an hour is too much. So we need to step away and let the child find another way to proceed on the path. Whenever we are giving stimulation that is getting longer and longer, it is a good time to step away and let the child go deeper and further on the inner path.

- However the child learns to go to sleep at night—the routine followed—needs to be recreated every evening. If the child awakens in the middle of the night, she depends upon the ritual being repeated again in its entirety. For example, if the parent lies with the child until he falls asleep, when the child wakens in the night, he wants this again. If the ritual for going to sleep is elaborate, this all becomes more complicated. Simple is better.

- A recommendation is that much of the bedtime ritual be moved out of the bedroom. After bath a child might start running around (balance and self-movement) as a step toward sleep. Wrestle, snuggle, run around, and read a story, as the child needs. Move into the bedroom for a two-minute ritual of candle and verse, then the parent moves outside.

When we put a baby down awake and he fusses a bit and moves, he is following the pathway inward to the life sense. Practicing this pathway gives the child independence to self-sooth. When a child pulls us along to be outer anchors, this shows us an undeveloped life sense.

Looking at Our Own Sleep Patterns to a Picture of this Pathway
February 7, 2015

Did you sleep well? Did you do anything before you went to sleep? Did you rub your face on the pillow? Did you stretch? There are also scrunchers. Did you scrunch?

Some of you must be gifted to lie down and be asleep in 30 seconds. Discovering oneself in this way can lead to a celebration of realizing that we do have methods of self-soothing when we are in a different situation. To come to the life sense, we have to be able to release from the outside world. We twist our mouth, cross our legs, etc., to bring attention into ourselves.

This presentation is still in the category of active work and research. This is an attempt to develop a way of looking and observing instead of following a set of rules. We can refine some of what we encountered last night. These are big concepts that call forth a lot of thinking. Last night was more thinking. Today is a sort of feeling day. Tomorrow will be a willing day to share practicalities of what we can do in our classrooms.

To review last night:

- Taste is related to nursing.

- Smell detects the presence of the mother and her milk. Even the smell associated with mother and milk is calming.

- Touch is satisfied by swaddling. Touch is about physically encountering things but also about feeling oneself change in relationship to the world.

- Balance is engaged when the child is being moved about by the parent, cradle, or rocking chair. Balance is also called the vestibular sense. But balance as Rudolf Steiner spoke of it is broader than the vestibular system. The term vestibular is more specific to balance as registered by the inner ear. We experience more than just physical balance in relation to the earth's gravity. This sense of equanimity operates on multiple levels.

- Self-movement relates to knowing that one has moved and where one's body parts are in relationship to one another. Self-movement is also called proprioception. But self-movement as we understand it is a broader, more all-encompassing term.

Reading Rudolf Steiner can be overwhelming in both content and thought. Steiner spent years thinking about and refining his observations before he spoke about these subjects. We do not know how many years he had been thinking and refining his perceptions before he got to the structure he presents in his lectures. He had already worked extensively before he came to his own clarity. Coming to our own clarity, coming to our own understanding is also a weaving back and forth.

The progression spoken of last night of the child maturing in outer movement development is accompanied by a simultaneous inward movement. These movements are unique to each *individual* child and family situation. When talking about these things, parents can start to feel guilty and incompetent. Things are different for different children. The guidelines shared last night are windows of opportunity for when a child can make a shift. Some children never need support to cultivate their life sense. They can settle in a state and rest there—the hierarchies are guiding in a harmonious way. If a family's first child is one of these, then the second will likely be very different. We have to adjust to each individual. Following this pathway will hopefully bring us to a point where we will have some idea of what to do in any particular situation. There are no "shoulds." What works for one child may be completely wrong for another child or family situation.

The doctor speaks out of a medical bias. People do not come to him to ask him to admire a child's beautiful life sense. Usually families come to him because the life sense is not unfolding well.

We have seen a puppet play with a little girl pushing and pulling on a rock set in her pathway. There are times and places where the child needs strong sensory experiences. For example, the child needs touch. For some children the body is big and the spiritual activity inside does not quite fill it out yet. A child I recently observed was always building houses; he built three during free play. He was in movement most of the time. He did not give hugs. If he had, they would have been big, strong hugs. His body is bigger than his sensing activity. In building houses (inside of which he had no interest to play) he was pushing in his physicality to meet his spiritual-sensing capacity.

The next day, in a different kindergarten, I saw two or three boys on the morning walk who deliberately walked into telephone poles to smack their bodies against. Some touch senses need that kind of reinforcement all the time.

In the classroom with the big, house-building boy, there was also a small, dark girl with a baby-doll mouth who watched the visitor very carefully. She frequently gets into confrontations with other children. This happens with almost every encounter, so sometimes she plays by herself. For her, her body is small and her sensing activity extends outward beyond her physical boundary. After the first boy had built a house and had moved on to build another one, this little girl came in and played very happily by herself with a veil over her head. She did not want to build the house, but she wanted to live in it. The boy wanted to build the house but not live in it. He wanted to be constantly doing. The girl has trouble coming to the sense of life because she is always guarded about what might come toward her. When there is a strong sensory need, this can stand as a stone in the path of getting to the life sense. If there is a stone in the path, we will often see difficulty with the life sense. When a child bangs into a telephone pole over and over, he is trying to educate his life sense. He is trying to sculpt his body. When we direct our attention to think to feel our socks, we are expanding our sensing activity. A child who is always thinking about socks and collars is constantly sensing and has no let up from experiencing. A child with overly awake sensing can be happy and at peace in her bed and is then able to pull her astral body in.

It is important to think about imbalances, because they can tell us why a child is having difficulty over and over again as a pattern. Then we can intervene to give the sensory input more support at another time.

Another day I saw a child who has had a complicated medical life so far. She got a triangular hollow block, wiggled almost like she was doing the twist, and then stood on the block. She was creating her own therapy. If there could be more opportunity for that child to have that block, this could be therapy.

Until these sensory needs are addressed, the path to the life sense can be blocked. With unmet sensory development, there will usually be an undeveloped life sense.

Let's say there is a child who needs a long time to suck. Is this bad? There are children who do need to nurse for years and years. There are children who need pacifiers for a long time. Some need the suck sensation for a longer time than they can nurse, longer than mom can tolerate. These children need more than a person can provide. With a child who needed taste and smell a lot, as a doctor one would try to move the child toward the next sense in the sensory progression. Go ahead and begin removing the binky, but also move toward supplying something further along on the progression. We can try to both give the child more of the sought-after sensory experience and also look to see where the child is stuck.

Where does the life sense go? In *The Riddle of Humanity,*[2] Rudolf Steiner gives a picture of a seven-foldness, inside the circle of the twelve senses, that is like the planetary movements, which are never static. The relationships of each to the other are constantly changing. This inner world is the realm of the life processes. The seven life processes are:

- Breathing
- Warming
- Nourishing
- Secreting / Separating going simultaneously outward and inward. Sorting may be a better word.
- Maintaining
- Growing
- Reproducing

In his book *The First Seven Years*,[3] Dr. Edmond Schoorel speaks of these life processes and gives other names for them as well. His terms for the metabolic processes are:

- Taking in
- Adapting
- Breaking down
- Sorting
- Maintaining
- Growing
- Bringing into being

These are important because everything we bring into ourselves, be it substances or experiences, has to go through these processes to make them our own. We can also apply these seven processes to the steps we go through with our thinking. Dr. Schoorel adjusts these seven steps to describe the thinking process:

- Taking in
- Recognizing
- Analyzing

- Questioning
- Combining
- Imbedding
- Recreating

We can also consider the progression of these life processes along with adult biographical development, with its characteristic nodes and crisis points, to enlighten our picture of adult human development. When development begins to stir, there is a kind of "itchiness." What was at peace is not anymore. Then, as the change comes closer, we can say, "I know what this is about." And we can stay at this stage a long time.

In the next step, something has changed and you can never go back. This is akin to nourishing/analyzing.

The secreting and sorting stage involves questioning. What is the right next thing? What must be left behind? What stays?

Then comes the stage of ashes, of maintaining. You feel that something is gone. You are exhausted from asking questions, so you just stop. It can feel like you need to be doing lots of things, and you are not doing anything. But it is really a time of grace. This stage can be so helpful. A person has to get to this place before growth can happen. This is maintenance—embedding, a planting-in, a quiet, holding place that allows something new to come forward. We live in a world where embedding is incredibly hard to do.

I heard a news feature recently about boredom. Should anyone ever be bored? The reporter said she has never been bored since she got a smartphone. "Boredom" is a kind of maintaining. Children need this. They are constantly encountering; they do not need more. They need to be able to take something in and just let it live.

As with eating, there has to be time of not eating. Our sense of physical hunger works really well if we eat and then don't eat for a while. If we give a child a snack, or continuously answer the child's questions over and over, we can never move through to the life sense.

One way to build maintaining is to establish consistent rhythms. This is one of the beauties of the Waldorf kindergarten. But even though we live in Waldorf communities, we can get pushed to "fastness." In a Waldorf first grade I recently visited, the speaking of the morning verse was fast. It is appropriate to meet the children where they are and then move to where they need to be led. We can begin at a faster tempo and then gradually lead the children to a calmer pace.

We live so much in orienting to the outside world that to have that removed makes us anxious. Children who ask questions all the time might be avoiding going to the life sense. The child's unspoken experience may be, "I don't know that I can get to the life sense, so I will do something else to keep from going on the path. Even negative attention helps me to know where I am." We need to create the space for the child to take these steps. We are always going through the seven steps. When we sing in rounds here in our conference and can create and hear the harmonies, it is like being able to tolerate the harmony of how these different activities are sounding together.

Morality lives in the limbs. Moving the limbs—intentional, purposeful activity—is the spiritual activity that allows us to morally experience the world. Holding open a heavy door to experience self-movement can be a more potent experience than going to an occupational therapist. The child can feel good about doing something that also serves others. The more that children can do real work, the more they will find the experiences they need in self-movement, balance, and touch.

The next stage we will consider is where the awakening to the life sense happens. We have so far been talking more about sleeping processes. We have been talking about the eye of the needle, coming to know oneself on the path to the life sense. We want to help the children be able to thread the needle. The individual can better encounter the outside world when he knows himself.

Bringing these Insights into our Practical, Daily Work with the Children

February 8, 2015

Today is the "will" day for us to take some threads from this weekend and begin to tie them together.

There is a progression during a conference. The first day, questions are about facts—"Did you just say?" "Did you mean…?" The next day come observations—"This is life sense, this is life sense. Is this the life sense?" Then the last morning come lots of questions about—"I have a child who…" In other words, "How does all this relate to my actual work?"

As the child is on the outward path, going out into the world, there is an accompanying inner movement (depicted by the chart we have been working with). We can envision a hand reaching in. Some children can reach only a little way in. As their motor activity gets outwardly bigger, their inner activity becomes larger as well. Eventually the child can reach the life sense. This matures into independent movement and the gateway through taste can fall away. As the child moves more toward self-movement, her dependence on smell falls away. We still have these connections but it does not have to be active and touched upon at every moment. We hope the child can roll and shake and move around so that she learns to self-soothe.

Whenever there is a step forward, there is also a regression. A new capacity awakens and the child is suddenly aware of being more independent in the world. This is exciting, but the child doesn't know to be excited. If a new sibling arrives and the child's relationship to the world has changed, there is regression. So the child goes backward a little. But the whole spiritual stream is carrying the child forward.

In the Karma lectures,[4] Rudolf Steiner describes how the spiritual hierarchies are active in our physiology. He says that there is a difference between the part we are aware of and the part guided by the hierarchies. To describe this spatially: if we were in water, the top of the head above the eyes would represent the part we are consciously aware of. The healthy unfolding of spiritual development is bathing us all the time. When a child expresses distress in a developmental moment, this is a picture of the child realizing that something new is coming that she doesn't know how to handle. As parents and teachers, we are inclined to try harder, to hold the children tighter, to protect them more in anxious moments.

We can give a child taste, smell, and touch experiences. We can give the child the opportunity to sense balance, but we cannot make them sense balance. No matter how much I love the child, I cannot do this for her. Somewhere in her there is a shifting point where she has to experience balance, self-movement, and life for herself. To create balance experiences, there is actually a machine like a giant gyroscope where the child is given intense sensory experience. We can give the child experience but cannot make the child be in it. We can provide the gateway, the pathway for it, but we cannot do the experiencing for them.

We can do the same thing with the life processes. We meet something consciously through nourishing but then we reach a point where we cannot logically go from one point to another. We have to stop at maintaining outwardly so something inwardly can manifest. In the grief process, when there is a loss and it hits us like a wave every moment, it is such a shock. Then we come to a place where it is not with us continuously. In time we come to where we can forget about it for a while. This can be bittersweet. But eventually we can still be holding someone spiritually in a new way. It is sort of like the liberated etheric forces for the seven-year-old. It has already happened before we realize it.

We feel the child's insecurity so we remove challenges. Then the child gets stuck a little bit. If the child is uncertain and those around him are uncertain, then the child really doesn't know what to do. Helicopter parenting is not healthy for the life sense. A time comes with a sensory needful child when everything the child needs cannot be provided from the outside. We can see with circle time, for example, that a child may need to practice outside of the circle time with an adult, away from the group, to learn to do it on his own. The child needs to make an inward change. At the nine-year change, the health of the life sense becomes incredibly important. The child feels isolated and desperately needs the security of the life sense. If we become primarily dependent on the outside world, that leaves us very open and vulnerable to influences from the outside because we don't know what will happen if we don't have that connection (i.e., the smartphone). This can lead to dependent relationships with people, with technology, with substances. The human being cannot find his home within himself. If the child has not found the way to the life sense by the time the teeth change, getting there will become a specific therapeutic activity.

So what do we do? We can create little homes.

- Child is used to having another person beside him to go to sleep. The child needs touch. We can give something to touch as replacement, such as blanket hugs, swaddling, lots of stuffed animals in the bed, layers of covers, tucking the bed in really tightly, for example.

- Co-sleeping/attachment parenting. What is the opposite of attachment parenting? Is it abandonment parenting? These words do not really describe what we are striving for. Are there times when the parent must be totally connecting to the child? Absolutely, but not exclusively. If there is attachment, there has to be unfolding as well. We can call this life-process parenting. There are cultures where everyone sleeps together in same bed and same room, and it works beautifully. We live in a culture where it is really easy to be bounced around and overstimulated in the world outside of home and classroom. In this kind of environment it is even more important to have one's own space in which to reflect and digest. If we are in a community where life is rhythmic and flowing, then culturally we are living in the life senses all the time. A child may ask why the adults get to sleep together. This is because we are able to sleep alone. But if we depended upon another for all of our orientation and security, it would not be good. If I cannot feel safe within myself and my interaction with the other, then I will avoid the other. As a doctor, I do not see children who have healthy life senses. I see those who have troubles. And these are helpful places to look for information and insight.

- Doing joint compressions (self-movement) is a marker to help the child remember where the destination of deep relaxation and sleep is, and this is a step on the pathway we are going along.

- When we have gone through our process of touch, balance, and self-movement, escort the child into the darkened bedroom and say "It is dark. It is time for sleep." Don't rock her until she falls asleep.

- A child with a history of trauma or sexual abuse is a child whose life sense has been disrupted. These children have extra needs, absolutely. Adoption is a biographical life-sense trauma. This child needs an extra-long approach. The same kind of progression would still be a goal. Some anchoring sensory behaviors may last a long time. We do for the child what is needed but we always hold in mind, "Where are we going?"

- Masturbation: The child is self-soothing. Assure that it is not a situation of abuse. Most of the time a preschool child realizes that this is a touch experience that feels different. Sometimes the child has a vocabulary that is beyond his understanding. What to do? Provide a safe and private place. Set a boundary by saying that this is private—not shaming. Shaming is not good for the life sense. If we put a boundary on it and it is not changing, what can we do? Give the child her own baby doll or something else to hold. Sexual stimulation does provide a short-cut to the life sense, but we want to give other touch experiences to the life sense that will be reassuring.

- To the child who asks questions all the time, reply, "I wonder?" Acknowledge the child and then give him something to do—peel a carrot. Often these children ask questions to establish connection, not to seek information or explanation.

In considering first-grade readiness, the life sense is an important criterion for children who are borderline. Some children are plenty smart and will do well academically, but lack a healthy life sense. They do well until the nine-year change or adolescence, and then they will fall apart. If we ask how the life sense was at school entry, and the experience at nine-year change and adolescence, we will likely find that these children are not as independent and depend more on their peers.

Rudolf Steiner says that we come into the life sense. There is a spiritual capacity that unfolds from each of the senses. For the life sense, it is the *spiritual experience* of *well-being*. For self-movement, it is the experience of one's *own free soul element; I feel myself free.* For balance, there is the capacity of equanimity, having inner tranquility. When the physical organ matures, there is an experience of a spiritual organ that lifts us up to a spiritual experience. With touch, that is an experience of feeling permeated by God. These are all worthy capacities and experiences to strive for through this pathway toward the life sense.

NOTES

1. Rudolf Steiner, *Spiritual Science as a Foundation for Social Forms* (Hudson, NY: Anthroposophic Press, 1986).

2. Rudolf Steiner, *The Riddle of Humanity: The Spiritual Background of Human History* (Forest Row, UK: Steiner Press, 1990).

3. Edmond Schoorel, *The First Seven Years: Physiology of Childhood* (Fair Oaks, California: Rudolf Steiner College Press, 2004).

4. See, e.g., Rudolf Steiner, *Karmic Relationships* Vols. 1-8 (Great Barrington, Massachusetts: SteinerBooks, 2015).

5. The Life Sense from the Perspective of Point and Periphery

Barbara Baldwin

February 5-7, 2016

Our rightful place as educators is to be removers of hindrances.
Each child in every age brings something new into the world
from divine regions,
And it is our task as educators
To remove body and soul obstacles out of the child's way,
To remove hindrances so that the spirit may enter
In full freedom into life.

—RUDOLF STEINER[1]

Introduction

Early in my career in curative education I felt drawn to the work of early childhood education: I wanted to experience what the children bring into the world from divine regions. A question I hold to this day is: How can we remain open in this modern world so eager to impose our expectations on children? How can we remain open enough to receive this wonderful gift of new spiritual impulses to carry us into the future? You kindergarten teachers are

97

blessed to be closer to the spiritual world through the children you teach. How can we learn from them and yet still be aware of their frailties and open to their needs?

When a child is born, the spirit, which was expanded in its pre-earthly life, gets compressed into this tiny frame, has to learn to orientate itself within this small body in the physical world. Dr. Hans Erhard Lauer, the first person to elucidate Rudolf Steiner's understanding that the four lower senses are actually a reflection of the child's pre-earthly existence, wrote:

> Everything we take in through the senses is more than mere sense impression. Through our senses we experience those spiritual forces which make us what we, as human beings, can become. The early experiences of the lower sense are an echo of prenatal experiences.
>
> The **Sense of Balance** is a reflection of our experience in the actual Spiritual world (the realm of the Zodiac)
>
> The **Sense of Movement** is a reflection of our experience in the planetary spheres
>
> The **Sense of Life** is a reflection of our experience in the etheric region that surrounds the earth
>
> The **Sense of Touch** is related to the formative effect of the external world on the human organism.[2]

In infancy the sensory experience is still unified and undifferentiated. As the three faculties of thinking, feeling and willing develop, the senses take on a more distinctly sensory character. Initially this happens unconsciously, but it can later be raised into consciousness. This process can clearly be seen when observing a small child: how he inadvertently touches the sides of the bassinet, which slowly triggers awareness. The action is repeated until it becomes an experience. Actions such as bumping into things and scratching are attempts to experience boundaries in the physical world—where perhaps the early experiences were somehow insufficient.

In this presentation we will explore the life sense within the context of the twelve senses, particularly how it reveals itself with all its frailties in children who have different learning needs and who may be in need of special education.

We will view various conditions of the senses in relation to the concept of point and periphery. This is a central concept in curative education and the motif of the meditation given by Rudolf Steiner to curative educators.

We will also view extremes of sensory activity, particularly in relation to the life sense, which we encounter in children today.

Foundational Concepts

Steiner originally spoke of only ten senses,[3] regarding touch and ego, or "I," as intrinsic to all sensory activity: every sensing is a form of touching and our ego is involved in every sensory process. This remains true;[4] however, he later distinguished these two as senses in their own right: the sense of touch gives us a boundary between self and world, and the sense of ego enables us to go beyond the physical boundary to an awareness of the other as a separate being. Touch and ego are deeply connected. The sense of touch conveys an awareness of where I end and the world begins, and at the same time gives an innate sense of security, of *being* within my own body. It separates us from the world and thus connects us to ourselves within our body. We find many disturbances in this area in children today, often manifesting in excessive touching of self and others, hitting, and scratching, which can be understood as an attempt to reinforce the experience of the body as a boundary.

Similarly, the sense of touch forms the basis for the unfolding of the sense of I and other. Steiner referred to this sense as the *Ich-Sinn*, the I-sense, which was translated as the sense of ego. This has led to misunderstandings and confusion between the activity of the ego— as in I do, I feel— and the sensing of the other as a separate entity.

To sense the other, we have to activate the sense of ego, we "sleep into the other and wake up to ourselves" in quick succession.[5] To do this requires the fundamental experience delivered by the sense of touch. Just as many children today have disturbances of the sense of touch, so many adults (as well as children) have a weakness in the sense of I or other: a lack of awareness, in some cases even a fear of invading another's space. This lack of awareness also expresses itself as rudeness, indifference, and lack of empathy—in some cases even as a total blotting out of the other.

This brings us to the fundamental distinction between doing and sensing, between thinking and perceiving.

In the infant, willing and sensing are inseparable; they only gradually become separate faculties. In *doing,* our will and metabolic-limb system are involved; in *perceiving,* our intention and nervous system are involved. Willing is instinctual, inherent from birth; it engages the musculature. Sensing and perceiving slowly awaken in the child through the effects of the environment. As the will activity permeates the body and comes under the child's control, the sensory system is freed into activity. In willing, an inner motivation moves toward the world; in sensing and perceiving, the world imprints itself on our being. Kindergarten teachers know that the young child is fully sense organ,[6] taking in all sensations from her environment. Perceptions make a deep imprint on the young and susceptible organs of the child.

Karl König points out the fundamental distinction between discrimination and integration. Discrimination is an analytical activity: through discrimination I learn to differentiate and the world becomes richer. Integration is a synthesizing activity: I bring things together, make a wholeness of parts, and in so doing the experience of my self becomes stronger.

> I remember as a child, walking and playing on the meadow, enjoying the feel and the smell of the grass and jumping into the pungent newly-mown piles of grass.

> My father, a gardener, one day taught me to distinguish
> the different types of grass and to recognize the differ-
> ent "weeds" as herbs. Suddenly, the greenness under-
> foot was no longer just "grass." It became a whole world
> of enormous interest, and I delighted in my new-found
> awareness and knowledge.[7]

We exist in a twofold relation to the world. On the one hand: I am my
world, I am at the center of my world and from this center I activate
my senses, which connect me with the world. On the other hand: the
world flows in through my senses and affects me unconsciously, yet
the more I become conscious of the world the more I can refine my
sense activity and thus become more cognizant of myself as separate
from the world—as a knowing and growing separate entity.

Many senses are already active *in utero*, but only when the child exists
in the world does it gradually wake up to the world of the senses: the
world enters the child's consciousness through the senses, and as the
sense impressions penetrate his consciousness, he activates his sense
organs and intentionally connects with the world.

The I-being of each one of us is the great integrator of the senses.
Without the "I," the sense world invades us. As the "I" awakens
through the sense activity, it is able to educate the sense organs and
their activity.

Point and Periphery

Point and periphery is the central theme of these talks. In many verses Steiner refers to this motif of the relationship between self and world:

> Through the wide world there lives and moves the real being of man;
>
> While in the innermost core of man the mirror image of the world is living.
>
> The I unites the two and thus fulfils the meaning of existence.[8]

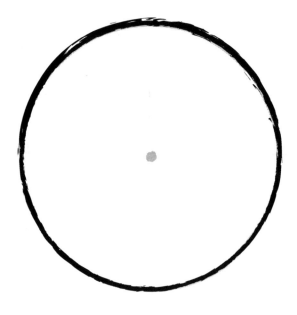

Diagram 1

Every sense has a central and a peripheral aspect, and this fact is essential to your work as kindergarten teachers. We are all obviously the center of our own lives, but both in our families and in our work, we form the periphery for our children. How we do this determines the level of protection or openness we provide. In the family, we have to grow with our children and be overly protective. In our kindergartens, we have to provide the level of protection and openness appropriate for each age group, and also for the temperament, constitution, and needs of each child. This task demands constant awareness and adjustment. We have to be grounded in our center, so that we can move our awareness to the periphery without losing the center.

Every morning we create the circle, a periphery which is at the same time its own center. Each child is her own center on this periphery. At the same time we create a center whose periphery is the room and the world. What happens to children who are unable to join in creating the circle? Do they experience this "intangible" element too strongly? Some throw themselves into the center, as though they cannot bear to be exposed on the periphery; others remain on the periphery and cannot let themselves become part of the little "center."

I have heard many kindergarten teachers say that children on the periphery are happy and prefer to be outsiders. As a result, some children have, with the teacher's blessing, remained on the periphery for their entire kindergarten career. But the truth for many is that they want to join in but cannot. As they adjust to the routine of the kindergarten, being in the periphery may be fine; but we must always inwardly include them and gradually also outwardly invite them into the circle.

As stated by Naoki Higashida, a Japanese poet who began to write as a 13-year-old boy with autism: "The truth is, we'd love to be with other people. But because things never, ever go right, we end up getting used to being alone, without even noticing this is happening. Whenever I overhear someone remark how much I prefer being on my own, it makes me feel desperately lonely."[9]

These children are stuck in their own little centers and can't find a way to connect. They can't move between center and periphery as most of us learn to do. They experience intense discomfort at the transition from home to school, from indoors to outdoors, from one activity to another. Many children today have such difficulties with transitions. The experience of these difficulties is conveyed through the life sense and may be expressed through behaviors like pushing and bumping, hitting and biting, or covering the ears and screaming. These behaviors express the feeling of discomfort arising in the life sense; they communicate to the world that the child does not feel safe, happy, or secure.

How can we respond? Find what this shy, sensorily insecure, defensive, or autistic child enjoys, what he *can* respond to, and begin there. Join him in repetitive play, so that he does not feel so alone. Join him in his little center. Realize that he can often participate from a distance, even though he seems to be ignoring you. Perhaps he can't show his participation through facial expression or eye contact, but do not give up on him or assume he does not understand.

At the other extreme is the child who throws herself into the middle of the circle, spoiling the togetherness and destroying the ambience. Basically every child would like to join in and be part of the group with the other children, would like to please her teacher and parents. She would if she could— but she can't. Some feel a constant agitation and restlessness, which drives them into action, when the rest of the class is silent.

Case study:

Josh was a "wild boy," always on the move, who pushed and shoved his way to get what he wanted. He talked with a loud voice, and any piece of wood would become a gun or a weapon, which he wielded indiscriminately, making loud, vulgar-sounding noises. How to deal with this disturbing factor in the kindergarten? The kindergarten director working with Josh met him each day with a rake or a broom. She greeted him with a smile, handed the tool to him, and invited him to help her with the "job" she was doing. That done, she'd send him to the wooded end of the kindergarten to "shoot the wild bear" or to catch the giant fish. There he could shout and wield his weapons, without endangering others, and got rid of some of his surplus energy by the time everyone came together for play time or morning circle.

It takes moral imagination to understand and deal with these children, so that we don't resort to isolation or even punitive measures.

Another example of this separation can be seen in children who want to speak but can't. Some can speak at home but not at school; some can speak with other children but not with adults; some fall silent the moment they step out of their homes. These children carry the diagnosis of selective mutism. Adults who have overcome their silence say that they find this diagnosis offensive. It is not a choice; they long to speak, but cannot. Teachers often report that they "won't" talk because they've heard the child talk to other children or their parent. This is not the case and one should not take it personally. These children long to chatter away like other children—and at home they are often loud and bossy—but outside the home, they are unable to make a sound. Their muteness is a silent expression that something is blocked between them and the world—often based on fear or anxiety. Only love, patience, and acceptance can help to heal the pain they feel at their exclusion. These children are usually extremely intelligent and often quite interactive; they just cannot speak.

Case study:

Lilly is a slender girl with light transparent skin and big eyes. She keenly observes everything that the other children do, listens to and enjoys stories, often smiles when another child is naughty. She clearly understands everything, is intelligent and usually plays quietly in a corner. She likes to help the teachers with little tasks. At home she is reported to be boisterous, loud, and dominating. Initially she is totally silent at kindergarten, following all routines, but never speaking or making a sound. When she needs something, she stands and looks, using her eyes to indicate that she needs the toilet or wants a drink. Gradually she is heard to hum some of the circle songs (mother reported that she knows them all and sings them at home) and with time joins in with all the gestures. Very slowly and quietly, she is able to join in. It would have been a fatal mistake to cajole, or even compliment her on her progress. This could have set her back completely. She might once again have become paralyzed by expectations. Quiet patience and acceptance helped to unlock the prison of the center and allow her to move more freely between self and others, between center and periphery.

Again, every sense has its central and peripheral aspect. Listening to a lecture, you can focus your auditory and visual attention on the speaker and screen out all peripheral information to direct your attention to what is important. We usually do this constantly without thought. Karl König gives an amusing example about the sense of touch which also includes the senses of self movement (body image) and life sense.

Imagine lying on a beach, the sun warming you from above, the sand warming you from below: you expand into a generalized sense of well-being. Suddenly you feel a tickling, which moves up your arm— an ant. You feel it progressing upward, but you don't want to lose the basking sense of warmth and wellness. However, soon the general sense is lost and you focus on the advancing ant.

Without moving any other part of the body or looking, your other hand swats it, finding the exact spot to catch the creature and toss it back into the sand. You resume your sunbathing at the beach.

How is this possible? At one moment you were totally lost in the peripheral experience of well-being; the next, your sense of life is disturbed by the itch, your sense of touch follows its progress, and your sense of self movement informs your other hand exactly where to swipe in order to catch the creature. Attention moves from peripheral to central awareness and back again to relaxation and semi-oblivion. The senses work together seamlessly throughout.

The Life Sense in Life

Let's look at the genesis of the life sense and come to an understanding of its disturbances. The life sense is already present *in utero* and is closely linked to the mother's sense of wellness. It is functional in its own right from the moment of birth; a sleeping baby radiates a sense of harmony and contentment. Conversely, as soon as the infant experiences any discomfort, hunger, or pain, the life sense leaps into action, sending messages of the disruption into this state of harmony, and the child cries. The sense of life gives information about the state of the body, not about the soul, so we must realise that when a child cries, it is externalising the bodily pain. Soul pain arises later. As Edmond Schoorel says in his excellent book about the first seven years of life: the sense of life mirrors the bodily functions, alerting us to anything that is not in order within the body, within the life processes.[10]

Early in life, any disruption of the life sense is overwhelming. The infant can't distinguish the different parts of her body, so any discomfort or pleasure is a whole-body experience. Just think of a baby feeding: she drinks not only with her mouth; fingers and even toes show their involvement and enjoyment. Similarly, pain for an infant is a total experience, giving rise to gut-wrenching screams until an adult can find and fix the cause. A toddler can usually tell that he has hurt himself, but not be able to point to the cause of the pain. Only gradually does this become more localized. By age four, most children can tell whether they have a headache or a tummy ache, or where they have hurt themselves after a fall.

Now, there are children whose sense of pain remains heightened. These children respond intensely to every discomfort. The smallest hurt or pain causes a major disruption in their sense of well-being. They cry excessively and long. They are demanding, need comforting, often need some outward form of first aid (cream or a bandage) before they can find a state of equilibrium again. In actual fact, these children rarely reach a state of equilibrium but live in a continuously heightened state of alertness and anxiety because they so often feel hurt, pain, and discomfort.

We know these children well in our kindergartens. In the mornings they cling to their parents, find it difficult to adjust, like to be close to the teacher. They generally don't move around much, preferring to stay in one place. They often whine and complain: "It's too noisy, too hot, too cold, too bright, there's not enough of this or there's too much of that…." They can easily get on our nerves because they are demanding and often need extra coaxing and coddling. What is going on here?

These children's senses are too alert. They feel too acutely. When any sense is overreacting, it affects the life sense. Any disruption anywhere will affect the life sense of these children—and initially they need our protection, our understanding, and our sympathy. Only gradually, through our understanding and empathy, can they learn to manage their pain and discomfort.

Case Study:

A large-headed six-year-old boy with blue eyes and curly blond hair talks with a pleasant and melodic voice and can express himself well—when he feels well. However, he often feels unwell, tires easily, seems to complain a lot, but can't really express himself well during these states. It's as though he goes into shut-down. Once, in a playground, he wanted to go onto a small rotating toy, but soon wanted to get off, not wanting to expose himself to the gyrations. He wanted on and off again several times, until the adult, losing patience, called him a "wuss," adding insult to injury. He really was trying to overcome his fear and discomfort caused by an oversensitivity in the sense of balance. The physical pain he was trying to deal with now had become soul pain as well. Though the adult quickly realized the shock and distress she had caused and apologized, the adult carried shame and guilt at having misread and mismanaged the situation for a long time. I know. I was that adult and for a long time I inwardly asked for forgiveness from my grandson, for this shameful lapse in my human understanding and empathy.

This incident taught me how easily and how often we do these children an injustice. They are so sensitive that they are often late with such things as bike riding and other skills that come naturally to most children. Their hypersensitivity causes discomfort, makes them anxious, and prevents them from engaging in activities in which they really long to participate.

At the other end of the spectrum of reactivity, we have children with a very high pain threshold. Very often they seem like a bull in a china shop: being "klutzy," blustering, bumping into things and people, pushing things over, talking too loudly and reacting too little. We know them well and often fear the disruption they bring into the kindergarten. We like things to be calm and orderly, but these children arrive with a bang. In some cases (though not all) they have a strong urge to play. They direct things and they know exactly what they want and will punch and pull to get things their way. When they fall, they never cry, don't seem to notice pain, and seem totally oblivious to any pain they cause others. Bumping into others gives them sensation. They are sensation-seeking because their life sense is under-responsive, so they do not receive the neural feedback they need.

Every child wants to belong, to be accepted and loved. It pains them not to feel the connection, yet they will often repeat annoying or painful behaviors because at least the pain gives them an experience. I knew a boy who fell and cut his leg to the bone but didn't notice it until other children screamed and pointed to the blood. His life sense gave him no feedback, so he was constantly in search of sensory experience—and this search was a danger to himself and a major disruption to the class.

These children, too, need nurturing, but from the opposite extreme. One needs to give them deep muscle experiences: rolling them in a blanket, kneading them like dough, rubbing and brushing their skin to awaken them to sensation. Then gradually soften the touch to bring them to awareness of themselves. Simple body geography, touching with playful slapping and scratching, rubbing, brushing, tapping, and stroking help them feel the enclosing boundary of their body. This helps them sense differentiation, so they can be drawn from the periphery into the comfort of their own center.

Each sense has its own pattern of growth and development, which is more or less the same for everyone, unless there is a disturbance. The disturbances may be of two kinds: either hyper—too sensitive; or hypo—under-sensitive. Hypo children don't experience their boundary and get lost in the periphery, as in some forms of ADHD. Those in the hyper extreme get caught within their own organism and can't connect (as in Asperger syndrome). Some swing between these two poles and this really confuses us. We see both in our kindergartens and both can be disruptive and should give us cause to pause and consider what is going on.

If we can recognize these extremes of behavior as aspects of center and periphery, we can find a new pathway to understanding, and develop new approaches to what appear to be "behaviors" but which are really disturbances in the life sense.

Point and Periphery Becomes Circle and Point in Curative Education

In 1924, Rudolf Steiner gave twelve lectures to a group of young doctors and educators that laid the foundation for what we know today as curative education.[11] Five introductory lectures are followed by content based on live child observations. These lectures gave practical indications for therapeutic education and deep insights and directives for the art of curative education. In the tenth lecture, he presents the meditation for curative educators, based on point and periphery, relating the exercise to the most profound knowledge of the human being. The theme of point and periphery, the relationship of what is within to what lives without, what works from one incarnation to the next, is fundamental to any work with children who have difficulties incarnating into their bodies. We cannot do this work without inner preparation. The point and periphery meditation is one tool to help us prepare.

Exercise:

Sit comfortably and relaxed. Now visualize a point. Make sure that you are really visualizing a point and don't let it disperse. A point is solid, compressed, contracted spacelessness. Now expand this point, but keep it as a point. Let the point grow without allowing it to become a circle, without letting it lose its quality of a point. See how far you can expand the point without allowing it to become anything other than a point.

Let that go.

Now visualize a circle. Round, complete, spatial, with inner and outer space, but mainly with an inner space and spaciousness. Now contract this circle, without losing the quality of the circle. Don't allow it to become a point. Maintain it as a circle, no matter how small it becomes.

Let that go.

Now imagine each of them again. Then gradually, very gradually, speed up the process of alternating between the two, without losing the essence of the initial exercise.

Once we become proficient at this, we can experience a natural movement between the two poles. We can learn to breathe into the movement between them: we can, with a small effort, let go of one and enter into the other, without getting lost or caught in either.

We live between these poles daily and can usually move with ease between point and periphery. Little children can't do this. As they grow and mature, most children develop focal and peripheral attention. However, some do not. They remain more or less imprisoned in one extreme. Some are unable to contract from the periphery to the center to gain self-awareness. Others are so caught up in consciousness and self-awareness that they can't relax or expand their sensing. Others can't move smoothly between the two, often having a tantrum before being able to change their orientation.

Now let us look at the Steiner's meditation.[12]

> In the evening, after we have lived the day in the world, we visualise a blue circle with a yellow point (see Diagram 2, upper image), and flow out into the cosmic blue of the night, with the thought "In me is God." In the morning, we converge toward our body, which we can experience as a blue dot (we have contracted into our bodies—astral and ego draw in from the periphery every morning to unite with the physical and etheric). This becomes our center when we awaken from our sojourn in the spiritual world, and we visualize the yellow circle and the blue point (Diagram 2, lower image), with the thought: "I am in God" and allow this thought to radiate throughout the day. This becomes clearer if we think of ourselves as always in the blue and God as represented by yellow.

Evening Meditation

Try to accustom yourself to
live into the consciousness:
In me is God. In me is
God—or the spirit of God,
or whatever expression you
wish to use, but please do
not think of this truth as
theoretical.

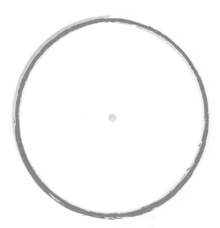

Morning Meditation

Let the knowledge that
I am in God shine
through the whole day.

Diagram 2

Finding the Spiritual Essence
through Paradox of outer Polarities

And now consider! When you bring to life within you these two ideas, which are then no longer mere thoughts, but have become something felt and perceived inwardly, have even become impulses of will with in you, what is it you are doing?

First, you have this picture before you:

In me is God

And on the following morning, you have this picture before you:

I am in God

The two figures are one and the same. In the morning, you have a circle (yellow) and a point (blue). And in the evening you have a circle (blue) and a point (yellow). You begin to understand that *a circle is a point*, and *a point is a circle*. You acquire a deep inner understanding of this fact.

Diagram 3

114

Then Rudolf Steiner draws a diagram to indicate the human being in the *Curative Course* (see Diagram 4) The head is shown with the physical body on the outermost layer (the skull), enclosing the cerebrospinal fluid (of the etheric body), which surrounds the nerves (of the astral body). The diagram places the ego of the human being in the very center—in the upper pole.

The same elements appear in reverse order in our limbs. The physical lies in the center of each limb (in the bones), surrounded by muscle, then blood, and finally the ego on the outside. With our body we express our ego through our movements. When we see someone walking towards us, we can recognize our friend by how her limbs move. When we see someone we know in a restful sitting position, we recognize the shape of his head and his profile, which has imprinted itself onto the physical. The "I" is hidden within. Diagram 4 depicts this aspect of point and periphery in the physical body.

A Curative Attitude: Observing the Life Sense in Devotion to Small Things

We have to learn to observe the details and the polarities between the head and the limbs. Steiner exhorts curative educators to pay attention to the detail, to take an interest in the minutiae of the expression of what is human, to devote ourselves without judgment to what is present. Kindergarten teachers and curative educators pay attention to these things in preparation for a child study; we also school ourselves to pay attention to these things on a daily and hourly basis, so that at any time we can recall every detail of the child's physicality, her movements, gestures, speech, and so forth. We must be able to live into the child's constitution, so that we have a sense of who she is from the inside—feel what it is to be large- or small-headed, fantasy-rich or fantasy-poor, and so on.

In the curative course, Steiner describes the head in its formation as a result of our deeds in former incarnations, and the thoughts we carry in our heads as related to the past. Our capacity for thought is something that arises from the past; whereas our will, our capacity to act, is directed to the future. Our thoughts are not products of our brain; they originate in the cosmic ether, from which we gather the etheric forces to form our etheric body. Thoughts, per se, can never be wrong; only our way of connecting and interpreting them can go awry. We can connect and interpret thoughts in original ways, but every thought we have has been thought before. Everything I say or write has been gleaned, read, or heard from someone before me. In our heads, Steiner says, we are acquisitive. We take each other's thoughts and put them together to write essays, give speeches, and make points. This activity rightly belongs in the upper pole. What happens if this activity is displaced and sinks into the area of will? In lecture 9 of the course for curative educators, Steiner says, "Then we become little kleptomaniacs."[13] If the "thieving," which has its rightful place in the head, slips into the realm of will, then we start to take, hold, and possess things that don't belong to us. If we make the effort to live into this state, then we no longer judge children who take things. It is no longer a moral issue; it is an experience for which we can feel empathy. We learn to deal with the situation with love and understanding.

I am often asked what to do with children who steal or take and collect things. In the lecture just mentioned, Steiner gave a wonderful description of the symptoms, causes and remediation of conditions such as kleptomania. He describes how morality belongs solely to the earth, and doesn't exist in the spiritual world. It is something we acquire here on earth through our will. Thus this type of acquisitiveness is also not primarily a moral issue, but an immaturity between the separation of the upper and the lower pole. Steiner then describes helpful remedies.

Understanding the Human Being

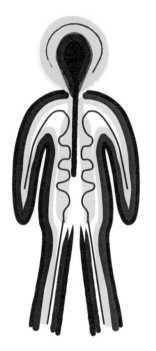

In envisioning or meditating upon the metabolism, we can imagine a "limbs figure" and a "head figure." In the human being this becomes a reality: the I-point of the head becomes, in the limb figure, the circle.

These two figures, these two conceptions, are one and the same, are not at all different from one another. They only look different in representation.

Red = Ego
Blue-Purple = Astral
Yellow = Etheric
Gray lines = Physical

Diagram 4-1

There is a yellow circle; here it is too! There is a blue point; here it is too!

One is a diagram of the head, and one a diagram of the body.

When the point claims a place for itself in the body, it becomes the spinal cord, and then the part it plays in the head organization is continued in the spinal cord. There you have the inner dynamic of the morphology of man.

Red = Ego
Blue-Purple = Astral
Yellow = Etheric
Gray lines = Physical

Diagram 4-2

Children Prone to Sensory Overload

There are children who seem to cope better if allowed to remain on the periphery. These are children who easily experience sensory overload—sounds, colors, and even smells are too much for them. They sometimes react with "inappropriate" behaviors, which are merely an immature response to overpowering messages from their life sense. Teachers must be alert to these reactions in their earliest stages: blinking, hands over the ears, squeezing the legs together, or even the touching the genitals. These early signs of overload are externalized messages from the life sense. We often don't pay enough attention to them until they develop into disturbances in the classroom.

If we are observant, we can also notice when these children look with interest, perhaps smiling as they watch the others play or even during the morning circle. These moments indicate when to move in and invite the child a little closer, away from the periphery.

In the morning, we may see these children walking around the periphery, gently touching, sometimes even handling objects briefly, then replacing them. It's easy for us to make quick judgments. Based on our prior learning about the senses, we may say they are seeking touch, so they must be hypo. This may be true and additional tactile experiences may help the child to further integrate their perceptions. However, we need to look *how* they touch. Sometimes touching is a form of orientation. Most neurotypically developing children take in the situation through their vision. They can look into a space and feel okay. However, many children today don't gain sufficient security from merely looking: they need to touch their way into the space, so they explore the room through touch. If we then forbid them to touch, they remain alienated from the space. They may need to do this every morning, because for these children each day begins with a sense of insecurity, as their life sense is on high alert. They need to feel all the objects again, to reaffirm the objects' reality and also their own physical presence, in this place, at this time, today.

It helps for such children to arrive early, so that they can feel the objects and get comfortable in the space before the other children arrive; then they can gradually acclimatize to the increasing level of noise and interaction. If they arrive when class is already in full swing, they have to accommodate to what is already there, which makes a much greater demand on their life forces and life sense.[14]

Steiner described children with obvious needs as *Seelenpflegebeduerftige Kinder*, or *children in need of soul care*. But life sense concerns may also reside, if somewhat hidden, in the average child. Through all children, we are given the opportunity to study and understand the subtleties of the body and the soul. Steiner states that all teachers should have an understanding of normal development;

and all educators of children with special needs should be familiar with both typical and atypical child development.

The onus is on us to *understand* these differences. Feeling a need to fix them is an outdated attitude. When we identify children as difficult and disturbing, we are actually saying that their behaviors are difficult for *us;* they disturb *us.* The *children* are not disturbed by their behavior—in fact many behaviors are simply coping mechanisms. Steiner says we must rid ourselves of our fear of differences, and learn to meet the essence of the other. He calls the concepts of normality and abnormality mere abstractions. When we try to drive out abnormality, he says, we drive out a piece of genius.[15] He rejoiced when he walked around the first Waldorf school and saw naughty children.[16] In such children, he said, the spirit is active. He stated that when he looked into the Akashic records, he saw that people of genius often had a previous incarnation in an incomplete or imperfect body; they needed to have certain experiences on earth that could only be had in an imperfect vessel that could not house the spirit in the normal way.

It is not our task to fix problems or to normalize children. Our task is to know, recognize, and understand children's hindrances, to help them step forward in fulfilling their own purpose and destiny in this life.

The Social Aspect of Point and Periphery

The principle of point and periphery lives in every aspect of our lives. It gives us the opportunity to bring awareness to situations and connections that would otherwise slip by unnoticed. When we are observing children, nature, situations, how does it reveal itself?

Point and periphery is also a social experience. In the Curative Course, Steiner gave therapeutic and medical indications to help children overcome their difficulties. Although these indications still hold true, in the past much of the work took place in isolation—between child and nurse or therapist. Today, we look at things more from a social perspective. How can we create inclusive situations, in which all children can find their place? How can we create situations in which everyone experiences growth and enrichment?

This may not always be possible. These days there is a wider range of capacities and challenges, and it is almost impossible to meet these within a class as whole—one must always be aware of and pay special attention to a child who cannot keep up or fit in. If we take a more social approach, we are looking for opportunities for learning and growing for all children, through the acceptance and inclusion of children with different abilities.

I believe that the ideal of inclusion lives strongly in most educators. But the reality of having children with diverse needs and behaviors in the classroom may be too much for many of us. We are torn between our ideals and reality.

How do we deal with this tension? These words by Heinrich Rombach might help:

> We don't have potential because we are perfect; our potential lies in our imperfections. Development might be seen as finding our way out of our imperfections.[17]

The children with differences give our other students, our classes, and our schools opportunities to overcome egoism, judgments, and habitual mental stances, to create new neural pathways of social acceptance and inclusivity. These children give us opportunities for social, emotional, and spiritual growth—if we only could have the courage to accept them. Just acknowledging that this is so is an important first step.

Challenging situations help us to grow, to become who we really want to be. We need to celebrate imperfections. To invite a little chaos into our lives helps us create something new.

We all exhibit some form of challenging behavior that we have learned, as normally functioning people, to hide, mask, or downplay.

We can do this because our center, our ego, can re-establish balance when it goes out of kilter and sets free our idiosyncrasies. Children with special needs cannot do this. The imbalances are too great and their egos are not sufficiently incarnated to redress the situation. Karl König describes disability as something primarily human.[18] Most disabilities belong to a specific phase of development that has become stuck or arrested, so that further growth and development is no longer possible without extra help. Illness and disability are imbalances or displacements of the natural harmony; we are constantly overcoming these quirks and setbacks. We may have difficulty in meeting the world in the mornings or coming to rest in the evening. Others need to have consistent physical order and regular schedules to feel well. If we notice these states in ourselves, we can rest, eat, or drink to restore our sense of harmony and well-being. What in us is an idiosyncrasy can become a disability in our children because they do not have the forces—are not well enough integrated in their thinking, feeling, and willing—to manage these imbalances. Their distress becomes their state of being—they cannot realign themselves.

Consider children with ADHD. Every day they get into trouble, often not knowing why. Every day they go to school, hoping that this day will be different, but having no idea how they could make it different. If we can understand and empathize, if we can meet them with respect rather than exasperation, we can say, "I know that you tried." That will make a great difference—to them and to us. They breathe a sigh of relief at being understood. Their life sense can for a moment be restored from the high alert state of "fight or flight"— which is their "normal"—and align for a moment with the state of "rest and digest," which is our state of harmony and relaxation. Normal lies in the gentle alternation between the two.

We have these children in every class and we will continue to get more. They are the casualties of our time: the rushed lifestyle, the pollution, the misplaced use of technology, the overstimulation, the nature deficit disorder, and so on. Some of them have a diagnosis or label, others do not. Children with all variety of "disorders" and physical challenges will ask to join our kindergartens and schools. How do we deal with their differences in our classes and kindergartens?

Children are smart and can see that one child needs more help, or is excitable and erratic and needs the teacher's calming influence. Most children intuitively accept this, and make natural adjustments. Some children perceive this difference but can't internalize it and so become bullies. We need to pay attention to these children because this inability to internalize difference may emerge as a difficulty in internalizing shapes and patterns that make up letters and words. Their behavior may be an early indication of a learning difficulty. Many children will openly ask the child: "Why can't you walk?" (or see or hear). This questioning is all right, and we shouldn't regard it as rude. We do, however, need to be vigilant that this questioning does not become mean or hurtful. Individual situations can be subtle, and the questions and answers may not be obvious.

While each case must be handled individually, as a general guideline it is not respectful nor helpful to tell the class "about" the child. That creates separation. We need to find ways to be inclusive, to talk about the child with the child present, so she is part of the conversation: "Penny is learning that—aren't you, Penny? Just like some of us are learning to tie our shoes." Our language needs to normalize and include the difference. Difference is normal; we're all different and we must learn to celebrate and make space for difference. Of course, one can tell stories of the child, gnome, or animal who was different and gifted in its own way. We also need to be prepared for questions and answer them openly. Questions and curiosity belong to healthy children. If we in any way suppress these qualities in our children, we stifle their growth and actually cause a contraction in their attitude to life and to their life sense. Here there should be expansion and interest.

The Health of the Senses

Diagram 5 presents an overview of the senses and their functions, organs, and gifts.

FUNCTIONS, ORGANS AND GIFTS OF THE SENSES

SENSE OF TOUCH – *awareness of physical boundaries, defining self and non-self*
    Organ – skin
    Gift trust

SENSE OF LIFE – *conveying feeling of well-being or unwellness*
    Organ – autonomic nervous system (particularly sympathetic nervous system)
    Gift –harmony

SENSE OF MOVEMENT – *proprioception; perception of own body movements*
    Organ – peripheral nervous system
    Gift – freedom

SENSE OF BALANCE – *perceiving uprightness and relation to external space*
    Organ – semicircular canals
    Gift – centeredness, inner equilibrium

SENSE OF SMELL – *directly connecting with periphery; air*
    Organ – nose
    Gift – morality

SENSE OF TASTE – *actively internalizing substance; fluids*
    Organ – tongue
    Gift – tastefulness (personal, cultural)

SENSE OF SIGHT – *overviewing visual space /perceiving light, dark and color*
    Organ – eyes
    Gift – insight

SENSE OF WARMTH – *balancing warmth and cold inside and outside the body*
    Organ – circulation with heart at center
    Gift – soul warmth, interest

SENSE OF HEARING – *differentiating between noise, sound, voice and tone*
    Organ – ear, specifically cochlea
    Gift – penetrate being-ness of world and other

SENSE OF WORD – *ability to recognize words and gestures as meaningful*
    Organ – pyramidal system
    Gift – opening to the Logos

SENSE OF THOUGHT – *understanding thoughts behind words*
    Organ – parasympathetic nervous system
    Gift – understanding spiritual content

SENSE OF EGO – *perceiving the ego of the other*
    Organ – the whole human form at rest with head at its center
    Gift – perceiving spiritual essence

Diagram 5.

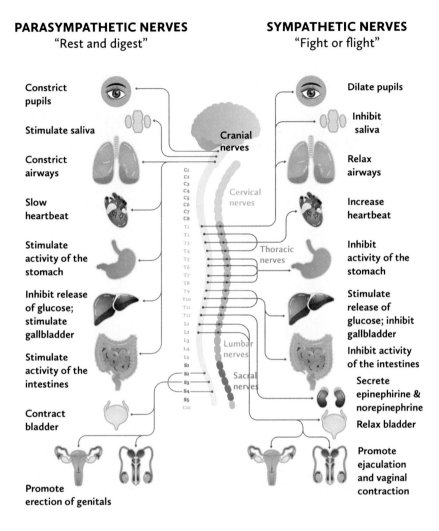

PARASYMPATHETIC NERVES
"Rest and digest"

SYMPATHETIC NERVES
"Fight or flight"

Constrict pupils

Stimulate saliva

Constrict airways

Slow heartbeat

Stimulate activity of the stomach

Inhibit release of glucose; stimulate gallbladder

Stimulate activity of the intestines

Contract bladder

Promote erection of genitals

Cranial nerves

Cervical nerves

Thoracic nerves

Lumbar nerves

Sacral nerves

Dilate pupils

Inhibit saliva

Relax airways

Increase heartbeat

Inhibit activity of the stomach

Stimulate release of glucose; inhibit gallbladder

Inhibit activity of the intestines

Secrete epinephirine & norepinephrine

Relax bladder

Promote ejaculation and vaginal contraction

Diagram 6

The life sense is the foundation for the sense of thought. Both the senses of life and thought have as their organ the autonomic nervous system (ANS), which is divided into the parasympathetic and the sympathetic nervous system. Diagram 6 shows the two systems and how each controls different responses: the sympathetic nerves give the warning signals of "fight or flight" to the life sense; each organ responds according to which part of the autonomic nervous system is dominant. For example, the pupil of the eye responds by dilating. Furthermore, if we look at the place of origin of each reaction, we see that the sense of thought originates in the cranial nerves (the vagus nerve), whereas the life sense originates in the organs themselves. *Image: VectorMine/Shutterstock.*

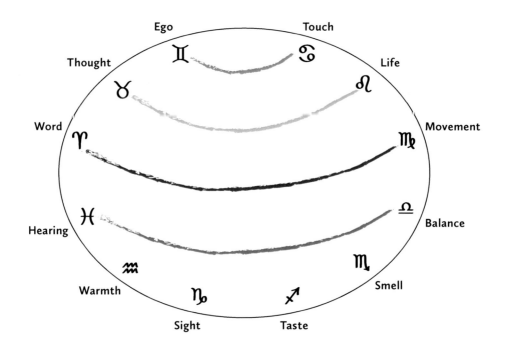

Diagram 7

Diagram 7 shows the relationship between the higher and lower senses. The life sense, which is deeply linked to all our senses, represents the whole human being: the upper, more energizing and wakeful; the lower, calming and less conscious; and the soul aspects of thinking, feeling, and willing. All of these must be in harmonious interplay for the sense of thought to unfold.

Diagram 6 offers a snapshot of human physiology related to the senses, and Diagram 7 relates the higher and lower sense to each other.

The sense organs are spread throughout the body, with their center in the nerve-sense system of the upper pole. Each sense organ is formed *in utero* for its specific function, yet it only awakens to full functioning if four preconditions are fulfilled:

1. Each organ must be fully developed in order to fulfil its role as a sense organ. A sense that is incomplete or physically deformed cannot serve as an instrument for receiving the sense impression.

2. The sense organ must be healthy. A head cold and a stuffy nose may infringe on the senses of taste and smell. Dairy intolerance may result in blockage of the ears. In these cases, the organs are not healthy and are unable to fulfil their role as instruments of perception.

3. The soul must be awake enough to be present in the sense activity. The organs may be fully formed and healthy, but they still may not serve the child if the soul is not sufficiently awake. The sense organs awaken the soul of an infant. But in certain forms of global, or overall developmental delay, this does not happen. The astral body is "asleep" and unable to respond to sensory stimuli. The child remains unreceptive to sound or light or touch until we can reach in and awaken the soul.

4. The "I" can direct attention into the sense organ. When we are tired, we may see and hear, but not comprehend. This happens when the "I" cannot direct its intentionality into the sense organs, as is often the case with ADHD. We have to will the organs into activity, directing our attention to focus on the intended object, sifting out peripheral information. We need to have the will to perceive.

In summary, there are four prerequisites for sense perception:

1.	A fully developed organ -	physical level
2.	A healthy organ -	etheric level
3.	A soul that is awake -	astral level
4.	The will to perceive -	level of the "I"[19]

Even when all these conditions are in place and each organ performs its function, no single, individual sense functions on its own. In a healthy person, multiple senses work together to convey the fullness of a sense perception. Here again, we can find irregularities; a child may rely too heavily on one sense to the exclusion of others and be deprived of the full sensory experience. Children who rely too strongly on their vision may miss verbal instructions from the teacher, as though they are deaf; yet their ears are fully functional. In such a case, the activity of the eyes can extinguish the activity of listening: the soul is totally absorbed in one sense perception to the detriment of all others. We often find this in children with certain learning difficulties. They are perfectly normal children in many respects, but their sensory activity has become so one-sided that they cannot function in a classroom with its many variables and distractions

The four lower senses develop during the preschool years and form the foundation upon which the higher senses develop. We all know that the lower senses are at risk in modern societies, due to our sedentary and passive lifestyle. Let us take a quick look at the senses in relationship to the disturbances we see in our kindergartens and schools.

Through the sense of touch, we perceive the surface and boundary of the physical body. Every contact with the outer world makes its imprint on the skin, which we register at a subconscious level. For some children this imprint is either too weak or too strong, as discussed above in "The Life Sense in Life," and the children respond accordingly to gain the imprint that will satisfy their sensory needs. Bumping, rubbing, hitting, biting, and scratching, among many other behaviors, can be signs of a disturbance in the sense of touch.

Through the sense of life, we perceive our state of well-being or its absence, based on the balance of the workings of the internal organs. Each of us registers our own state of well-being upon waking every morning and can take the necessary steps to deal with an experience of imbalance. In young children, the life sense is still a very generalized sensation. Not feeling comfortable and comforted in this realm can cause a real disturbance in their ability to participate. These may be children who complain a lot. A disturbance in any sense will affect the life sense, so if children's senses are too open, the life sense is under constant attack.

The sense of self movement provides us with a sense of where our body is in relation to itself. Just as our mouth seems to know what word to form to express our thoughts, so the movements of our hand anticipate an action.[20] Many children get too much or too little feedback from this sense, and are unable to move with the grace and fluidity that we expect in a kindergarten-age child. Children love to move; movement is their medium. But some children always seem to miss the mark. They knock things over, break things, are clumsy and ungainly, and are generally slow to develop fine motor skills. A careful look at their sense of movement will reveal their distress.[21]

The sense of balance tells us about the relationship of our body to the external world. With this sense we perceive our uprightness or any deviation from the upright position. Many children today have a disturbed perception in this sense. This can lead to a reluctance to engage in physical movement, or an almost manic need to move in order to get feedback from the space around them

With these four lower senses, the child takes hold of his physical organization. We can observe this wonderful process in infancy as the little child goes through the stages that lead to standing upright and walking. By the time children come to kindergarten, we expect these lower senses to be more or less integrated and in the process of refinement. However, ever-increasing numbers of children have not completed this process due to a disturbance of these bodily senses. We need to devise songs, games, and exercises to help the children to complete this process.[22] These four senses are trained by the body and for the body. This means that they develop through the activities of the body; and the more the senses are engaged, the more integrated in the body the child becomes.

The four middle senses have less to do with the body and more to do with connecting to the world through the awaking soul. We share the world with other souls, whereas our connection to our body is our own. We respond with sympathy or antipathy to the outside world. We have likes and dislikes in the realm of smell, taste, color, temperature, and even sounds. Here, too, we see disturbances—preferences can become obsessions and aversions. We often see this with foods, which is normal for a short phase of development. But if it continues over a longer period, it is a sign of a sensory disturbance, and the child needs help to move forward. The middle senses connect us with the world around us. If they become directed towards the body and self-gratification, they are disturbed. When these senses are functioning well, they teach the child to know his own soul, because they recognize the soul qualities in the environment.

The higher, more cognitive senses connect us to the spirit world—to the other. The sense of hearing, like the other senses, is already present at birth. The three highest senses, word, thought, and "I," are entirely dependent on education—in the broadest sense. In order to develop, they require the presence of other human beings. In saying this we can immediately intuit the level of damage that is caused by technology and screen time. Many children today are obsessed with their smartphones and tablets. In our regular routines of the Waldorf kindergarten, we do much to alleviate the sensory shortfalls that may result from this preoccupation. However, we know from recent research[23] that certain deficits are appearing that are attributed to screen use: a growing number of children do not understand gesture, facial expression, or the inflection of the voice (all connected to the sense of word); they hear what we say and understand the individual words but not the message (sense of thought). Some children are oblivious to the presence of others, treat others like objects, or are unable to empathize when another child is hurt (sense of other). Here again, we must rid ourselves of bias and judgment, perceive the disturbances in these senses, and activate Rudolf Steiner's pedagogical law: to engage with knowing intentionality so that our interventions can be really effective.[24]

Disturbances of the Senses

To really understand children with special needs, we need to look not only at the functioning of their senses, but also at their disturbances. If we understand the senses in their fullness, we will have a vital tool for meeting the needs of all children. Many behaviors and difficulties that we see in children today can be understood through the senses.

During the developmental stages of childhood, the sense organs are gradually awakened and can take hold of and assimilate the impressions coming in. Who is taking in and assimilating? It is the "I" or ego of the child, gradually awakening from within, stimulated by the sense world from without. As already mentioned, the senses help us to differentiate and discriminate the world around us and, in so doing, assist in the integration and the incarnation of the individual. The ego is the great integrator, enabling each sense organ to monitor and regulate what comes in, so that it can be assimilated and integrated.

However, in many of our children, the ego cannot fulfil this task. It cannot filter what comes in. For some children, too much comes in through one or more of the senses. Too much information, too many impressions invade the child's inner space, and she becomes defensive. The child wants to screen out some impressions. These children are hyper in one or more of their senses. If, on the other hand, the ego cannot take hold of the sense impressions at all, if the stimuli from the senses do not reach the child, the impressions are insufficient and the child seeks for more and becomes sensation-seeking. These children are hypo in their sensory life.

Let us look at how this plays out in the sense of touch.

The well-functioning sense of touch gives a sense of boundary, of containment, of belonging. If this sense is hyper, the child experiences too much sensation, cannot screen himself from incoming stimuli, and becomes what we call tactile defensive. Some children

131

say that their clothes are itchy and irritating. Parents have to cut off all labels for this reason. In class these children will avoid being in the midst of things, will go to the end of a line, and will play on the periphery, all to avoid being bumped into or inadvertently touched. All touch hurts. Even a small bump hurts. The child experiences it as painful. That is her experience and you can't argue with that. In extreme cases, any touch hurts; every little bit is too much. It is so painful that the child withdraws from almost any contact—unless she initiates it and controls it herself.

How different it is with the child who is hypo in the sense of touch. He is not getting enough sensation and is always craving more: he bumps into children and objects so he can feel himself and his boundaries; he likes pile-ups, lying on other children—without any sexual connotations, just needing to feel his physical self. He squeezes people's hands, thumps, hits, and scratches. He's not trying to be annoying; he just really *needs* these sensations.

For the hyper child, everything hurts; for the hypo child, nothing is enough.

With the life sense we perceive our state of wellness or otherwise. If we are healthy we feel well, and the life sense doesn't give us much feedback. We take our wellness for granted. As adults, can cope with things and make inner adjustments if something is slightly amiss.

For a child who is hyper in the life sense, any variation or surprise is upsetting and unsettling. It is as though she can't really settle into life: it's too warm or too cold; the food is too much or too little; her clothes are too tight, too loose, too itchy; the light is too strong—and the list goes on. When we ask her to participate, she needs time to adjust, to prepare herself. Life is hard for her. Because she complains about everything, people get annoyed with her. She then feels alone, unloved, and misunderstood, and she often gets teased. These children have a hard time, which can continue into adulthood. Even then other adults often get impatient with them. Yet they are just taking care of their existential needs. We must remember that if any sense is in imbalance, the general sense of well-being is affected. These hyper individuals often become sensitive, perceptive adults, keen observers who notice and attend to details as valued collaborators. They have empathy—probably because they have suffered so much. They create safety in being self-protective and seldom get hurt.

By contrast, children who are hypo in the life sense are a danger to themselves. They are often hypo in many other senses as well, so they often get hurt. They have a very high pain threshold, which means they don't notice warning signals that keep most of us safe. Because many sensations don't really register with them, they seek more. They don't have particular likes or dislikes, tend to eat whatever is in front of them, and eat too much, even if it's too hot or too cold. They often don't know what to wear—they dress too warmly in summer and not warmly enough in winter. They can get enthusiastic, then lose interest quickly. They don't sense when they're tired, so they keep going when they should rest. Then they make mistakes. They are easily confused and are often misunderstood.

The senses of self movement and balance are closely linked, so we will deal with them together.

Every movement has an effect on the balance of the whole organism. Even the smallest movement of the hand changes the subtle equilibrium of the body. In early childhood, when the senses of movement and balance are still developing, the child cannot yet adjust and easily falls over when reaching for something. As the senses mature, children become able to engage differently, their whole vestibular system coming into play when needed. Children who are hyper in their senses of movement and balance register every little change in their system, are easily overwhelmed by sensory input, and are reluctant movers. They play quietly in a corner, avoiding the activities of the group, and often like to stay close to the teacher or close to the wall. They prefer the periphery, even if they enjoy watching the activity in the center.

In one kindergarten, two children, an active boy and a tentative girl, were neighbors and friends. At home they regulated their play and adjusted to one another. In kindergarten the boy was very active, at the center of everything, and the girl played quietly on the periphery. On the day I visited I witnessed the following: the boy was directing the play—moving tables and chairs with much noise and ado, piling them high and making a ship with a look-out tower. Meanwhile the girl played quietly with cloths and ribbons. When the ship was ready, the boy fetched the girl. He helped her climb to the top of the tower, where he had placed a chair for her. From that safe position, she was able to be part of the game, sitting happily and safely away from the masses, without feeling threatened. This is a beautiful illustration of the hyper/hypo polarity, and a beautiful example of sensitive inclusion on the part of the children.

Caring for the Carergiver – Caring for Ourselves

We cannot close a discussion of the life sense without talking about caring for the carer. Obviously, as parents, we need to take care of ourselves. We need a partner or wider network as a supporting sounding board for our questions, problems, and frustrations. As teachers, we can be interested in and caring toward parents. But our primary concern must be the children in our care and their growth and well-being.

We cannot deal with challenging children unless we are grounded in ourselves, attending to our own self care. We often talk about parents and children not having good boundaries. We need to consider our own boundaries.

During the pioneer stage of a school, everyone is involved with setting things up and getting things ready: teachers, parents, grandparents, all together as co-workers, become friends and share energies to create the school. Then school begins and the teachers become "the teachers" and the parents become "the parents." We have to learn to set boundaries, accept our respective roles, and put process and procedure in place. This is an important step that takes time and thoughtful, respectful conversations. If this doesn't happen and roles remain unclear, confidences are broken, things can get very messy, and deep and unresolvable hurts can arise.

This is especially so if a child begins to show delays or developmental difficulties. Parents have left their school because their child was no longer accepted by the other parents. Teachers have been overwhelmed by worried parents.

There can be friendships, but clear boundaries need to be established: a teacher needs her privacy, both in time and space. There need to be set times for conversations and feedback outside of school hours.

We do set up limits and boundaries in general ways already. But in the case of children with special needs, there need to be clear procedures that are mutually understood and respected. It may be a good idea to have a journal in which both parents and teachers can succinctly record anything unusual that happens at home or at school. There needs to be agreement about regular meetings to assess the child's progress set on the calendar well in advance. If these forms are set and adhered to, it is easier to maintain healthy boundaries. As teachers, we must consciously step into our working space in the morning, and consciously step out of it in the afternoon. We leave school knowing that the space will be ready to step into the next morning, and we can let it rest for the evening.

Learning to care for the caregiver, that is, learning to take care of our own life sense, requires attention. Being fully present for our family at home, just as we are for our children in the kindergarten, is quite demanding. Our professional persona is so different from our private one. So what are the golden rules for teachers to nurture their life sense?

- Pay attention to the transition between work and home life.

- Be fully present, wherever you are, in everything you do, even when relaxing. As Karl König said in the early years to the co-workers of the Camphill community: "When in the garden, be a gardener; when in the classroom, be a teacher; and I would add, when at home be a spouse, parent, homemaker; when in a meeting, be a meeter; when with yourself, be yourself."[25]

- Set a rhythm for your life and breathe life into that rhythm.

- Take joy in being alive.

The life sense conveys to us a sense of wholeness. The foundation for the life sense lives in the etheric forces of growth and rejuvenation. We need to consciously nurture these forces, and we do so through enlivening all our senses. The more alive we are in the life of our senses in general, the stronger the life sense can become. Let us cultivate health and equanimity and meet life with the fullness of our trust in the spiritual world.

Raphael's masterpiece, *The Transfiguration*, provides us with a beautiful image of point and periphery, both in its wholeness and in its parts.

At the bottom of the painting, a group of people is gathered around a youth in the throes of an epileptic seizure. Everyone is so focused on the youth that the radiant figure of Health, in the foreground, goes totally unnoticed. All eyes are on the drama, the facial and body gestures all depicting excitement and vexation. Like the youth, the onlookers have succumbed to a state of excarnation: they point to the center (the youth) but their own center is empty. But if we look closely, we see a striking connection between the youth and Health, who is pointing directly at his heart, their two bodies molded as one. We all carry health within us, and it is our task to promote health within ourselves and in the world.

Rafael, The Transfiguration, *1516-20 (Pinacoteca of the Vatican Museums).*

In the upper part of the picture appears the Risen Christ—the force and the source of health. If we only pay attention to the news of wars, lies, and politics, we can get caught in the doom of destruction, not noticing the beauty of the natural world, the goodness in the world. The forces of rejuvenation are all around us.

Rafael, The Transfiguration, *detail.*

You, who from the light of heaven
Descend into the darkness of earth
To reveal spirit light
To enkindle spirit warmth
To call forth spirit strength
In the struggle of existence.

You through the warmth of my (our) love
Enlightening thinking
Calming feeling
Healing willing.

Because you are rooted in the Spirit-heights
And working in the grounds of Earth
You will become Servant of the Word:
Illuminating the Spirit
Realising Love
Strengthening Existence.[26]

NOTES

1. Rudolf Steiner, *The Spiritual Ground of Education* (Great Barrington, Massachusetts: Anthroposophic Press, 2004), lecture 4 (GA305).

2. Hans Erhard Lauer, *Die Zwölf Sinne des Menschen* (Basel: R. G. Zbinden & Co, 1953), ch. 3. Author's translation from the German.

3. In 1916 Rudolf Steiner referred to the senses as a twelve-fold unity in writings and lectures collected in *The Riddle of Humanity: The Spiritual Background of Human History* (Forest Row, UK: Steiner Press, 1990) (GA170) and *Toward Imagination: Culture and the Individual* (Hudson, New York: Anthroposophic Press, 1990) (GA169).

4. Here we have to distinguish between touch and sensing. I-touch is different from the sense of touch. When I touch, I reach out and seek contact with the world; in sensing, the world makes an imprint on me. (In the case of the sense of touch, the external world makes an impression on the tactile sensors below the skin. They are compressed, causing the sensation we call touch.) This arises through the nerve-sense system (NSS) of the upper pole. Similarly my sense of myself, my identification with myself, is an active state, whereas the sense of I or other is an activity of the NSS. We sense the other and in sensing the other, our own self is in a certain sense eclipsed. See Rudolf Steiner, *The Foundations of Human Experience* (Hudson, New York: Anthroposophic Press, 1996), lecture 8.

5. Steiner, *The Foundations of Human Experience*.

6. On the child as sense organ, see Rudolf Steiner, *Soul Economy* (Great Barrington, Massachusetts: SteinerBooks, 2003) (GA303); on the soul imitating the surroundings, see Rudolf Steiner, *The Child's Changing Consciousness and Waldorf Education* (Forest Row, UK: Rudolf Steiner Press, 1988) (GA306).

7. Karl König, *Being Human (Heilpädagogiksche Diagnostik)* (Hudson, New York: Anthroposophic Press, 1989), p. 37.

8. Rudolf Steiner, *Verses and Meditations* (Forest Row, UK: Rudolf Steiner Press, 2004). p. 59.

9. Naoki Higashida, *The Reason I Jump* (New York, Random House Press, 2014), p. 27.

10. Edmond Schoorel, *The First Seven Years* (Fair Oaks, California: Rudolf Steiner College Press, 2004), p. 135.

11. Rudolf Steiner, *Education for Special Needs: The Curative Education Course* (Forest Row: Rudolf Steiner Press, 2015) (GA317).

12. With kind permission from Karl Kaltenbach, founder of Warrah Village in NSW, Australia, for this elegant presentation of Steiner's meditation.

13. Steiner, *Education for Special Needs*, lecture 9.

14. In some kindergartens, children with additional needs are invited to join the class a little later than the other children, so that the class has already established its routine. I suggest that sensitive and vulnerable children visit the classroom during the holidays to get a feeling for the space when there is nobody around (except the teacher). They can then gradually spend short periods of time with the group to acclimatize, before being fully admitted to the class. In this way they get to know the classroom, before they get to know their classmates. These decisions must be taken individually, according to the need.

15. Steiner, *Education for Special Needs*, lecture 1.

16. Schoorel, *The First Seven Years*, p 243.

17. Heinrich Rombach (1923-2004), a German philosopher at the University of Würzburg, Germany, quoted in a lecture by Prof. Rüdiger Grimm in Dornach, Switzerland, October 13, 2002.

18. König, *Being Human*, ch. 1.

19. Schoorel, *First Seven Years,* ch. 4.

20. Observe yourself: if you want to pick up a pencil, your hand places itself in anticipation of the pencil; if you want a drink, your hand will form itself in anticipation of the size of the cup. This is the result of the working together of the senses of sight, balance, and movement in conjunction with our will.

21. For example, observe how the children hold hands in the morning circle: do they look at each hand as they grasp, or do they seem to know where their hands need to go; do they squeeze too hard, hurting the next child? This isn't necessarily malicious: it may be that their sense of movement cannot gauge the correct pressure.

22. It is best to do these things with the whole class, rather than to single out a particular child for therapeutic exercises. This is the social aspect of therapeutic education: everyone gains in growth and awareness physically, emotionally, socially.

23. Liraz Margalit, Ph.D., "What Screen-Time Can Really Do to Kids' Brains: Too much at the worst possible age can have lifetime consequences" (*Psychology Today*, April 2016), *www.psychologytoday.com/us/blog/ behind-online-behavior/201604/what-screen-time-can-really-do-kids-brains*

24. Steiner, *Education for Special Needs*, lecture 2.

25. See Karl König, "Leading Thoughts," at *www.karl-koenig-archive.net/mission.htm*.

26. Author unknown, usually attributed to Karl Schubert, first curative teacher, appointed by Rudolf Steiner.

Selected Bibliography

Aeppli, William
> *The Care and Development of the Human Senses* (Edinburgh, UK: Floris Books, 2013)

Ker, Ruth
> Editor, *From Kindergarten into the Grades,* (Chestnut Ridge, New York: Waldorf Early Childhood Association of North America, 2014)

Köhler, Henning
> *Working with Anxious, Nervous, and Depressed Children* (Chatham, New York: AWSNA, 1995)

König, Karl
> —*A Living Physiology* (Bolton Village, UK: Camphill Books, 1999)
> —*Being Human* (Heilpädagogiksche Diagnostik) (Hudson, New York: Anthroposophic Press, 1989)

Lipson, Michael
> *Stairway of Surprise: Six steps to a Creative Life* (Anthroposophic Press, 2002)

Neufeld, Gordon
> *Hold On to Your Kids: Why Parents Need to Matter More than Peers* (Toronto, Ontario, Candada: Vintage Canada, 2013)

Schaefer, Signe Eklund
> *Why on Earth?: Biography and the Practice of Human Becoming* (Great Barrington, Massachusetts: SteinerBooks, 2013)

Schoorel, Edmond
> *The First Seven Years: Physiology of Childhood* (Fair Oaks, California: Rudolf Steiner College Press, 2005)

Steiner, Rudolf
> —*Anthroposophy (A Fragment)* (Hudson, New York: Anthroposophic Press, 1996)

—*The Boundaries of Natural Science* (New York: Anthroposophic Press, 1983)

— *The Child's Changing Consciousness and Waldorf Education* (Forest Row, UK: Rudolf Steiner Press, 1988)

—*Education as a Force for Social Change* (Hudson, New York: Anthroposophic Press, 1997)

—*Education for Special Needs: The Curative Education Course* (Forest Row: Rudolf Steiner Press, 2015)

—*Education of the Child in the Light of Anthroposophy* (Forest Row, UK: Rudolf Steiner Press, 1981)

—*The Essentials of Education* (Great Barrington, Massachusetts: Anthroposophic Press, 1997)

—*Foundations of Human Experience* (Hudson, New York: Anthroposophic Press, 1996)

—*Karmic Relationships* Vols. 1-8 (Great Barrington, Massachusetts: SteinerBooks, 2015)

—*The Kingdom of Childhood* (Hudson, New York: Anthroposophic Press, 1995)

—*A Psychology of Body, Soul, and Spirit* (Great Barrington, Massachusetts: Steiner Books, 1999)

—*The Riddle of Humanity: The Spiritual Background of Human History* (Forest Row, UK: Steiner Press, 1990)

—*The Roots of Education* (Hudson, New York: Anthroposophic Press, 1997)

— *Soul Economy* (Great Barrington, Massachusetts: SteinerBooks, 2003)

— *The Spiritual Ground of Education* (Great Barrington, Massachusetts: Anthroposophic Press, 2004)

—*Spiritual Science as a Foundation for Social Forms* (London: Rudolf Steiner Press, 1986; Great Barrington, Massachusetts: Steiner Books, 1986)

—*Start Now!: A Book of Soul and Spiritual Exercises* (Great Barrington, Massachusetts: SteinerBooks, 2004)

—*Toward Imagination: Culture and the Individual* (Hudson, New York: Anthroposophic Press, 1990)

—*Verses and Meditations* (Forest Row, UK: Rudolf Steiner Press, 2004)